THE
seminary

---

student

---

writes

THE
seminary

---

student

---

writes

DEBORAH CORE

St. Louis, Missouri

Cover art: © Photodisc, Inc.
Cover design: Elizabeth Wright
Interior design: Elizabeth Wright

This book is printed on acid-free, recycled paper.

Visit Chalice Press on the World Wide Web at
www.chalicepress.com

10 9 8 7 6 5 4 3 2 1   00 01 02 03

Library of Congress Cataloging–in–Publication Data

Core, Deborah.
    The seminary student writes / Deborah Core.
        p.   cm.
    ISBN 0-8272-3447-3
    1. Christian literature–Authorship. 2. Academic writing. 3. Seminarians.
I. Title.
BR117 .C67 2000
808'.06623 – dc21   00-009050
                                                              CIP

Printed in the United States of America

*This book is dedicated to my fellow students
at Lexington Theological Seminary,
whose journeys I have been privileged to share.
I am blessed to be part of your community.*

Contents

Abbreviations

AB	Anchor Bible
ABD	*Anchor Bible Dictionary*
BETL	Bibliotheca ephemeridum theologicarum lovaniensium
BTB	*Biblical Theology Bulletin*
CD	Cairo Genizah copy of the *Damascus Document*
Gen Rab	Genesis Rabbah
JSOT	*Journal for the Study of the Old Testament*
LD	*lectio divina*
LXX	Septuagint
Mek. Exod.	*Mekilta Exodus*
NJBC	*New Jerome Biblical Commentary*
NRT	*La Nouvelle Revue Theologique*
NT	New Testament
OT	Old Testament
1QS	*Serekh ha-Yahad* or *Rule of the Community* from Cave 1
11Qtemple	Temple Scroll
Str-B	*Kommentar zum Neuen Testament*

Preface

The Seminary Student Writes is the outcome of a search. In 1992, after more than twenty years as a teacher of writing, I began taking seminary classes part-time. Getting into the content of seminary classes, I looked for a seminary-oriented book of preprofessional writing support such as exists in most other graduate academic areas. When I realized that no such book existed, I began to think that my experiences as a seminary student and as an English teacher of many years might enable me to fill the gap. I discussed my plans with Dr. Bonnie Thurston of Pittsburgh Theological Seminary, and her support encouraged me to go forward with the project. Other writing commitments prevented her from being as involved as I had hoped she could be in the actual writing of this book, but her generous sharing of ideas and resources has been a great help.

In the fall of 1998 I was asked to tutor my fellow students at Lexington Theological Seminary in writing. This opportunity was quite helpful to me in working on this book; I encountered much more directly the kinds of challenges students were facing, and I also had a chance to converse with the faculty about seminary writing. I am deeply grateful to all the faculty of LTS and to all my fellow students for what they have taught me, for the life of faith they have modeled, and for their gifts of community, prayer, friendship, and laughter. Special thanks go to Dr. Sharyn Dowd, now of Baylor University, for her commitment to excellence in writing, and to Dr. Margaret N. Ralph, seminary adjunct professor and secretary of educational ministry in the Catholic Diocese of Lexington, for encouragement and an eagle-eyed reading of the text.

Dr. Jane McAvoy encouraged me and worked with me on this project over many cups of coffee, and her writing-intensive classes have taught students that the act of writing can help them discover what they believe. Our work together in these classes shaped much of the content of this book, and our collaboration on an article, "Writing Discernment in Theological Education" (*Teaching Theology & Religion* 3, no.1 [2000]), describing our experiences was most helpful in pulling together ideas about the role of writing in this discipline. I am also grateful to the Wabash Center and the Lilly Foundation for grant support that enabled me to spend part of the summer of 1999 on this project.

I am deeply thankful for my colleagues at Eastern Kentucky University, who have made my work a vocation and who have taught me, over the years, most of what I know about writing and pedagogy. Professor Terry Culross, a reading specialist, kindly offered me insights on chapter 3. Dr. Joe Pellegrino provided invaluable computer expertise and developed the computer-oriented information in chapter 4. Special thanks go to Dr. Bonnie Plummer, chair of the English Department, an extraordinary writing teacher, colleague, and friend. Finally, a special note of appreciation to my secretary, Mrs. Virginia Hunt, whose steady kindness, humor, and efficiency brighten my days and who went out of her way to help me with this endeavor.

My family have been an unfailing source of faith and support during this project, as they have been throughout my life. Special thanks go to my mother, brothers, and sister for their encouragement and love. I am also grateful for the support of my Richmond "family"—my prayer group, Martha Brown, Beth Dotson, and Joan Adkins.

Dr. Jon L. Berquist, academic editor at Chalice Press, was insightful, thoughtful, and patient in handling this project. His suggestions have strengthened the book substantially; my thanks go out to him and to all at Chalice Press. I appreciate their confidence in me and their understanding the need for this work.

CHAPTER 1

Why Write?

In this book, you and I are beginning a journey together. As seminary students, thinking about journeys is something we do a lot. We think about all the journeys of the people of God in the Bible. We think about our relationships as journeys. We think about our life with God as a journey. We think about our years in seminary as a very special part of our lives' journeys—a special part with its own gifts and demands. Our time in seminary offers us an unparalleled faith community and also a world of new challenges, challenges to develop our faith and our intellects.

One aspect of those challenges, for many of us, will be the need to do reading and writing on a level we've not encountered before. The very tools of seminary education may seem more like obstacles or adversaries for students who have been out of the classroom for a while, or who simply lack confidence in their abilities. This text is intended to aid you in meeting the challenge and to support you on this journey. It is my hope that you will come to see reading, and especially writing, as tools for your growth.

A helpful companion will be a *journal.* If you've ever tried keeping a journal, you know that it can be a wonderful resource, providing comfort and insight. Whether we write about our internal or external worlds, we are gaining benefits and preserving our thoughts and experiences for future reflection. A further benefit is that a journal gets you in the habit of writing! If you don't currently keep a journal, I encourage you to start one now, today. Some will wish to use a computer journal, whereas others will prefer a simple notebook. People have different ideas about what a journal should look like and what kinds of things should go in it; you should go with whatever you find comfortable. Elsewhere I'll make some suggestions to you about keeping a journal, but right now, I'd like you to use your journal to do a little thinking about the act of writing.

What is writing to you? Is it a time of grace, when you are able to experience the word of God through your words? Or is it a time of struggle, when you are like Jacob wrestling with the angel and emerging with a blessing? Or is it a time of despair, when you wish only to be done with a very alien task? When you have writing to do, whose biblical story comes to mind? To understand our lives as writers, let's begin by taking some time to remember writing experiences. In your journal, jot down your answers to these questions:

1. What is your earliest memory of writing?

2. What are some positive responses you've received from your writing?

3. What are some negative experiences you've had with writing?

(Hints for using the journal: Begin with today's date and give specific details.)

One purpose of this book is to help you see the blessedness of the act and accomplishment of writing. For many of us, writing began as a creative and exciting action; as little children, we were thrilled when we could make lines and circles into block letters, and then make those block letters into our own names. As time went on, we learned to use writing to convey our learning and to tell our stories. As we mastered the skill of writing, it belonged to us, a tool we held in our hands.

Then, for many of us, our relationship to writing changed. It became a dreaded chore, and part of our self-image was that we were just no good at writing. We dreaded classes that had lengthy paper assignments or even essay tests.

How did this change happen? I suspect that several events and attitudes work together to corrode our confidence in ourselves as writers. Many of us began to be judged for correctness in our writing long before our ability to *be* correct could catch up. Effective writing has many aspects, and correctness is an important one, but it is not the only one. However, many of us were at some point scolded for making mechanical errors in writing, errors we were perhaps helpless to avoid. Meanwhile, what we did well went unremarked.

Or perhaps it was not correctness but the content of one particular paper that was criticized. Because writing is an intimate, subjective, and personal action, we generally find it much harder and more painful to deal with criticism of our writing as opposed to, say, a low score on an objective exam. An attack upon what I've written can feel very much like an attack on me.

If we identify ourselves as "bad" or hopeless writers, for whatever reason, our problems continue to grow, because the need to write never goes away. While we can pretty much leave behind our terrible experience of trying to master college algebra or physics, we cannot do the same with writing! G. Lynn Nelson has written a persuasive and helpful book on journals called *Writing and Being: Taking Back Our Lives Through the Power of Language.* For our purposes here, I might retitle his book *Taking Back Our Language Through the Power of Our Lives.* With some prayerful reflection on our experiences, we can indeed come to realize that the worth and blessedness of our whole lives may be reflected and understood through our own written words. We can, all of us, appropriate for ourselves what Kathleen Norris calls "the hard grace of human language."[1]

Therefore, I suggest that we begin to think about writing from a religious viewpoint and open up this part of our

---

[1]Kathleen Norris, *Amazing Grace: A Vocabulary of Faith* (New York: Riverhead Books, 1998), 138.

intellectual (or even emotional) lives to the transforming power of God. Let's explore the idea that the communicating, writing part of our lives–regardless of our past experiences–can be enriched, blessed, and used by God.

Now take a moment to go back and read what you wrote in your journal. Are any of those memories still shaping how you respond to writing tasks today? When I look back, I recall Mr. Romick, one of my high school English teachers, who told me that my writing was thoughtful and persuasive. I recall how encouraged I was by Mr. Romick–even when he pointed out the shortcomings in my work. But I also remember another teacher, for whom no work was good enough. And I recall the sinking feeling of getting a paper back from this teacher (I'll call him Mr. X), who would just mark a *C* at the end of each of my essays, with no comments to show me how to improve. In Mr. X's class I felt that writing well was a mysterious process, one that always eluded me. The *C* marked me as just average, unable to communicate as well as I wanted. While I was under Mr. X's influence, I saw myself as a mediocre writer at best, with no hope of improvement. Soon after, though, I encountered Mr. Romick, and my self-image improved substantially.

(If you are using this text in a classroom setting, I hope you will take some time now to discuss in small groups your responses to my three questions. If you're using the book on your own, you might want to find a friend to work with.)

Now that we have remembered a number of our writing experiences, what do we do with them? I suggest that we first take a few moments to consider how these experiences, positive and negative, are still with us in our attitudes. When facing a writing task, do we tend to revert to the self who felt hopeless? Do we recall the empowering and encouraging moments? Let's accept those past experiences for what they can teach us and for what they don't teach us. In my case, I need to recognize that Mr. X didn't really teach me anything about my writing. All he did was give me a flat assessment; he did not help me understand my weaknesses or find ways to improve. His methods caused me to feel powerless and stupid–feelings none of us enjoy. So I need to recognize when those Mr. X–rooted moments of cosmic self-doubt occur in me, and I need to banish those ghosts. And if this remembering has made me angry with him, I also need to do some forgiving! Similarly, my act of remembering calls me to pray in gratitude for Mr. Romick and others who fostered a healthier attitude in me.

(Spend some time now reflecting and writing about what these memories have revealed to you. Do you understand more now about your attitudes toward writing?)

The kind of writing you have just done in your journal is meditative writing. It has the goal of recording and nourishing us. We do this kind of writing simply for ourselves, not necessarily for communication to others or to feed into other sorts of writing. Although journal writing is not the focus of this book, we should recognize that it can be an excellent companion on our journeys: It can help to cleanse and develop our personal lives, thus freeing us for other tasks, and it can develop skills that will transfer to other work.[2] In other words, if we value our writing skills or our spiritual lives, journal writing is never a waste of time!

Many contemporary writers have reflected upon the profound ways that our past and present may be intertwined meaningfully through the experience of writing. Dan Wakefield, for example, believes that "the past isn't just a set of experiences that are irrevocably set, like concrete blocks that can be hauled up out of memory and the unconscious to be reexamined and better understood."[3] Rather, he argues, we may constantly reinterpret our experiences, not just understand them better: "Since our past only exists now in our own mind—it only 'lives' in our recreation of it—our changed experience of it becomes the reality, and in that sense we really do have the power to change the past."[4] John Leax recounts the same sort of experience: "What I've set down, I've discovered as I've written. What

---

[2]The physical and emotional benefits of journal writing are discussed in Joshua M. Smyth et al., "Effects of Writing about Stressful Experiences on Symptom Reduction in Patients with Asthma or Rheumatoid Arthritis," *JAMA* 281 (1999): 1304–9. For more ideas about journaling, see "Further Resources" at the conclusion of this chapter.

[3]Dan Wakefield, *The Story of Your Life: Writing a Spiritual Autobiography* (Boston: Beacon Press, 1990), 22.

[4]Ibid.

remains to be written, I must discover as I write."[5] For Leax, writing is an essential tool for understanding the relationship between past and present, and language, he says, "is the foundation of my knowing and my being known."[6]

G. Lynn Nelson believes that we do more in writing than just record what we are already aware of: We actually grow in our knowledge; we create.[7] Often, traditional Christian language or thinking suggests ways in which we are God's partners in creation (for example, in becoming parents). Here, we may begin to see ourselves as similar to Adam, giving names to creation and thereby comprehending it more fully. All our life experiences are somehow gifts of God, and when we seek to know them and ourselves more fully through the gift of language, we are surely acting respectfully toward the complex blessedness of our lives.

Natalie Goldberg, a Buddhist, speaks of writing in language that parallels the Christian experience. She claims that "each time we sit down to write we have to be willing to die, to let go and enter something bigger than ourselves."[8] This is worth thinking about. What holds us back as writers? Whatever it is, we need to let it go, be willing to take the risk and "die" to ourselves and enter into the great mystery of creating. Let's praise God for this gift, this chance. And let's pray that any fears we have will be lifted and that our blessed voices may come out clear and strong in everything we write.

Further Resources

The books I've listed here are only a small sampling of what has become a genuine growth industry. As cultivating a spiritual life became a driving force in the self-improvement line of the publishing world in the 1980s and 1990s, so did books about the recording of that life. The books listed below

---

[5]John Leax, *Grace Is Where I Live: Writing as a Christian Vocation* (Grand Rapids, Mich.: Baker Books, 1993), 26.

[6]Ibid., 32.

[7]G. Lynn Nelson, *Writing and Being: Taking Back Our Lives Through the Power of Language* (San Diego: LuraMedia, 1994), 9.

[8]Natalie Goldberg, *Long Quiet Highway: Waking Up in America* (New York: Bantam Books, 1993), 93.

have been selected because they offer a variety of "takes" on a spiritual approach to writing. Some are specifically Christian and some are not, but all are worth a look.

Baldwin, Christina. *Life's Companion: Journal Writing as a Spiritual Quest.* New York: Bantam Books, 1991.

Cameron, Julia. *The Vein of Gold: A Journey to Your Creative Heart.* New York: G. P. Putnam's Sons, 1996.

Cheyney, Arnold B. *Writing: A Way to Pray.* Chicago: Loyola University Press, 1995.

DeSalvo, Louise. *Writing as a Way of Healing: How Telling Our Stories Transforms Our Lives.* San Francisco: Harper Collins, 1999.

Dorff, Francis, O. Praem. *Simply SoulStirring: Writing as Meditative Practice.* Mahwah, N.J.: Paulist Press, 1998.

Elbow, Peter. *Writing Without Teachers.* London: Oxford University Press, 1973.

Foehr, Regina Paxton, and Susan A. Schiller, eds. *The Spiritual Side of Writing: Unleashing the Learner's Whole Potential.* Portsmouth, N.H.: Boynton/Cook, 1997.

Goldberg, Natalie. *Long Quiet Highway: Waking Up in America.* New York: Bantam Books, 1993.

_____. *Writing Down the Bones: Freeing the Writer Within.* Boston: Shambhala Publications, 1986.

_____. *Wild Mind: Living the Writer's Life.* New York: Bantam Books, 1990.

Klug, Ronald. *How to Keep a Spiritual Journal: A Guide to Journal Keeping for Inner Growth and Personal Discovery.* Minneapolis: Augsberg Fortress, 1993.

Lamott, Anne. *Bird by Bird: Some Instructions on Writing and Life.* New York: Pantheon Books, 1994.

Leax, John. *Grace Is Where I Live: Writing as a Christian Vocation.* Grand Rapids, Mich.: Baker Books, 1993.

Macrorie, Ken. *Telling Writing.* 4th ed. Westport, Conn.: Boynton/Cook, 1985.

Nelson, G. Lynn. *Writing and Being: Taking Back Our Lives Through the Power of Language.* San Diego: LuraMedia, 1994.

Offner, Rose. *Journal to the Soul: The Art of Sacred Journal Keeping.* Salt Lake City: Gibbs Smith, 1996.

Progoff, Ira. *At a Journal Workshop: Writing to Access the Power of the Unconscious and Evoke Creative Ability.* Rev. ed. New York: G.P. Putnam's Sons, 1992.

Simons, George F. *Keeping Your Personal Journal.* New York: Ballantine Books, 1978.

Wakefield, Dan. *The Story of Your Life: Writing a Spiritual Autobiography.* Boston: Beacon Press, 1990.

CHAPTER 2

Beginning and Beyond

By now, we should have a better sense of what writing is all about and what it can do for us. With that understanding, it's time for us to look specifically at seminary writing tasks and responses to them. As always, let's begin this task with prayer. *Holy One, you wrote my name in the palm of your hand before time began. You commanded the prophets to write down your will for your people. Please let me, as I write, share your love and grace and wisdom through my words.*

Take a moment now to think about this semester, and list the writing challenges that face you. List all that you can think of, and be as specific as possible. What does your list look like? It may include things like these (I've lettered them for ease of discussion to follow):

Church history
    A. Fifteen-page term paper
    B. Essay exams
    C. Two reading reports

Intro. to ethics
  D. Annotated bibliography
  E. Weekly reflections
  F. Short research paper

A HELPFUL TIP

I've always found it helpful to make a "map" of each semester, a one- or two-page calendar on which I write due dates for important assignments or other time-consuming obligations. Planned travel and such may also be included. With the aid of this calendar, I can readily see not just my daily obligations but the flow of my time. I may not be able to alter the fact that two long papers are due the week after I've been out of town for a conference, but at least I can plan to avoid the worst of the time crunch. I pencil in the blocks of time when I expect to work on various projects and try to keep to that schedule. Beginning earlier than I need to is one key to being successful with this plan. If I begin a week early and all goes well, I'll have the project done a week early. Nothing wrong with that! On the other hand, if I begin "on time" and there is some sort of emergency, as there so often is, then my work will be late, and I'll have to finish it in such a way that I'm frustrated and dissatisfied with it. The professor may be, too. *Not* a good outcome.

Common sense tells us that not all seminary writing tasks will be alike; a look at the above tasks gives a sense of how very different they may be. To begin any writing task well, we have to think about what it's asking for and anticipate its demands and opportunities. This sort of thinking is the first stage of the writing process.

What Is the Writing Process?

Most writing happens as the result of a three-part process: we plan, write, and rewrite. These stages are not absolutely sequential, however. Sometimes we decide to write before we have completed our plans—we learn where we're going by going there. Sometimes we stop to ponder an awkward sentence and fix it before continuing. Sometimes we plan, write, then revise our plan, then write some more. Writing teachers refer to this nonsequential approach to the writing process as *recursive*. Perhaps when you were in school, teachers encouraged you to employ the writing process in a wholly sequential fashion, with formal outlines and such. In this way, these teachers sometimes elevated the process above the product and failed to recognize the rich and diverse ways writers can discover, create, and communicate.

It is certainly true that for some writers, the old three-stage method works well. But in recent years, writing teachers have become more flexible in teaching "the process," recognizing that successful writers work with the process in quite varied ways. It's important to appreciate and respect this variety of method. The process is a simply a tool. If I hire a carpenter to build a deck for me, I assume he'll show up with the proper tools to do the job. Part of being an effective worker is knowing what tools one needs and how to use them efficiently. There is no one "right" method. If your writing process works for you, yielding a solid product with a reasonable amount of effort, it's a good process. The job of the writing teacher, then, is not to mandate a rigid process but to introduce the writer to patterns, allowing each writer to choose what works for him or her.

With that bit of philosophy in mind, let's move on. The remainder of this chapter will suggest ways to work with planning, writing, and rewriting. You'll get some principles to guide you and some tools to help with trouble spots. And you'll be encouraged to assess what methods you are using now—to get to know yourself as a writer—and then do some fine-tuning, or perhaps make major changes, depending on those assessments.

Now take a few minutes to write in your journal, answering these questions:

1. For most writing assignments, do you think that you spend more time than you should to get an adequate result?

2. What steps of planning do you usually use?
3. Are you more comfortable writing quickly and then going back to make small changes, or do you prefer to stop to revise sentences and correct errors?
4. Do you ever get back a paper with lots of mechanical errors marked and realize you could have caught them?

In chapter 1 we saw how the journal can help you understand how you *feel* as a writer; these journal entries should help you move forward in another way, teaching you about how you *work* as a writer and what needs you may have. With those thoughts in mind, let's move ahead and look at the writing process itself.

Planning

Call it planning, prewriting, getting ready to write, or whatever else you like, but be aware that all writing projects involve some of it. When I make a simple grocery list, I do some planning: I always list produce items on the upper right corner of a sheet of paper, meats and dairy items on the bottom right, and everything else on the left. The purpose of my planning is obvious: It will help me move through the store with less backtracking. If I usually bought lots of frozen foods, I would probably make a special place on the page to list them. We wouldn't ordinarily think of "planning" a grocery list, and indeed, it is not something I reinvent every time I make a list, so it hardly feels like a plan. Nonetheless, my decision to divide my grocery list is a kind of plan, and it is a good one because it works effectively to speed my task. *A good plan is any plan that helps to create a satisfactory product in a reasonable length of time.*

Seminary writing projects are a bit more complicated than my grocery list. So, what else is involved in planning and preparing? Let's look at some ideas and options.

First, the plan should arise out of the project. It's probably impossible to develop a one-size-fits-all writing method. The amount and nature of the preparation we do will arise out of the needs of the writing. As you will see in appendix 2, essay exams pose special writing challenges in that they require very specific information, and they need to be done speedily. You can and should do some kind of planning (as you'll see in that appendix), but it will be different from what you do for a fifteen-page term paper. And what you do for a two-page reading report will be different from what you do for the term paper.

Our projects are different, and our mental processes are different. As you read this chapter, you will probably discover that some of the ideas I offer will be useful, while others won't work for you or will speak to parts of the process with which you are already comfortable. My intention is not to treat you as blank slates but rather to suggest some writing scenarios and potential responses. With that in mind, let's look at some projects and approaches to get ideas about how planning can work for them, and for us. To begin, let's go back to our list of an average semester's projects for two classes:

Church history
   A. Fifteen-page term paper
   B. Essay exams
   C. Two reading reports

Intro. to ethics
   D. Annotated bibliography
   E. Weekly reflections
   F. Short research paper

Let's begin with E, the weekly reflection papers for the ethics class. Your professor has asked that each week you write a one- to two-page essay looking at a current ethical issue, personal or public, through the perspective of Christian ethicists whom you've been studying. The assignment does not seem difficult, but when it comes time to write, you feel stuck. You sit and stare at the paper or computer screen and wonder where to start.

And this is where a *planning strategy* can ride to the rescue. When you don't know where to start and can't think of anything, step one is to think of *three* things. Maybe you can't think of one ethical issue to discuss, but I'll bet you can think of three. Sound odd? Try it. So now you're thinking something along the lines of *Well, there was that segment on* Dateline *about the cost of saving the lives of very premature babies. And then there was that situation last week with Craig and his boss...and now that I think about it, I had that really interesting discussion with Joan about whether it's morally wrong to be overweight!*

It's good to *write down* the three things; don't just let them go through your mind. If the phone rings or something else comes along to distract you, you'll have the record of what you were thinking. Also, writing the three things down is, after all, writing, and it primes the pump.

Now you have three possible subjects for your reflection paper. How on earth did you get three, when you couldn't even get one? The answer is simple. Many of us are paralyzed by perfectionism. I can sit for hours trying to think of the one perfect, illuminating topic. Such thinking puts incredible strain on me, and as time goes on, the topic choice of course gets more and more important because of the time I've poured into it! But if I have to come up with three possible topics, well, two of the three can be total losers, so the pressure of perfectionism is removed. Furthermore, if I have to come up with three ideas, I am more likely to dig deeper into my thoughts and experiences. Instead of looking for the one perfect thing to write about, I'm looking for a number of things that I've experienced and observed.

I call this method *the rule of three,* and you'll be hearing more about it as we go on. As you have seen, the rule of three can help break down writer's block and encourage us to voice our ideas. Try it.

Let's return to the ethics reflection paper. You now have three pretty good ideas for your topic. Choose one of them as the most promising for your paper—let's say, the one about the cost of saving premature babies. Remember, if you do some further thinking and find that one doesn't pan out, you can go back to one of the other two. But usually our instincts are effective guides, and the first one you choose will be likely to work for you.

Now what? Now that you have a potential topic, it's good to look back and review the assignment. For this one, the professor has simply asked you to take an issue and look at it through the perspective of the ethicists you've been studying, and to do this task in one or two pages. You hope to do this in a unified, thoughtful essay.

So you've got a topic. Are you ready to write? Probably not. Most of us, even for a brief paper, need more time to plan. Without planning, we may easily fill two pages, but we may just ramble, failing to make important points.

In order to write a thoughtful, unified essay, most of us need to articulate *where* the paper is going and *how* it's getting there. Good writing has a purpose, and it usually achieves its purpose by carrying out key ideas. What will the purpose be for this writing? It's often helpful to *write the purpose down in a sentence.* A purpose sentence focuses your thinking in helpful ways. This sentence usually, but not always, appears early in your essay. For this assignment, your purpose sentence might be something like, "This paper will look at the ethical issues of the cost involved in saving the lives of very premature babies." Sounds okay. But as you look at the sentence, you are thinking about the other issues raised—the potential low quality of life and the suffering that these newborns experience—and you think that other ethical issues besides cost are involved. Do you have space, in two pages, to deal with more than the issue of cost? Maybe. You don't need to decide right this minute. You try revising the sentence so that now it reads, "This paper will look at the ethical issues involved in saving the lives of very premature babies."

How do you know if your purpose sentence is a good one? There are ways you can *check your purpose sentence for effectiveness.* A good purpose sentence will have these qualities:

1. It should not simply be a statement of fact. Facts don't give us direction. They close conversational doors in writing, whereas an effective purpose statement will open doors to development. A statement like "Christianity and paganism both existed in Europe in the fourth century" is not going to give a writer much direction for a paper. On the other hand, "Christianity did not defeat paganism but rather absorbed it" is an argumentative statement that demands development.

Not all purpose statements will be strongly argumentative, but all should suggest a direction: information to be offered, problems to be explored, or understanding to be expanded.

2. A good purpose statement will be restricted to the extent that it can be effectively supported in the amount of space you have. The statement above could not effectively be handled in a brief paper. However, restrictions of time and space do not mean that you must abandon a subject you want to pursue. You can always trim it down to a manageable size. To deal effectively with the topic above, you might restrict it to one single aspect. "The history of hilltop shrines suggests that Christianity did not defeat paganism but rather absorbed it" might work as a purpose statement for a brief paper on this church history subject.

3. A good purpose statement will provoke questions. The reader (and here you put yourself in the reader's position) wants to know more; you can imagine a reader asking, "What makes you say that? Why do you think that? What proof is there for that contention? In what ways might that be true? What's the other side of that argument?"

At this point, the ability to *make your sentence into a question* will serve you well. It not only lets you check your purpose sentence, but it also helps you with your next writing task. The answer(s) to your reader's question will show you how to *organize your writing.* To illustrate this idea, let's return to the earlier topic, the short reflection paper for your ethics class.

The purpose sentence we generated was this: "This paper will look at the ethical issues involved in saving the lives of very premature babies." While this statement does not announce a viewpoint or present a strong argumentative angle, the very nature of the topic probably means that the paper will have the character of an argument. The initial question arising from the purpose statement is something like, "What are the ethical issues involved in saving the lives of very premature babies?" So we list those issues. How many should we list?

Again, think of *the rule of three.* Try coming up with three answers. You may find more than three later, or you may decide just to focus on one or two of the answers, but start by thinking about three. Working with this topic, you come up with something like this:

1. Huge investment of dollars and medical resources. Should they be expended in this way?

2. Suffering of the newborns. Shouldn't they be allowed to die peacefully?

3. Don't parents have the right to have everything possible done for the baby?

Notice that the answers themselves generate other questions, which seems appropriate considering the subject.

What's next? Remember that you are asked to apply the thinking of the ethicists you've been reading to these problems. So now you look back through your reading notes and find thoughts that will apply effectively. You decide to use Seán France's comments on biblical morality, and then Lisa Cahill's procedures for making moral judgments.

To complete your organizing, you have some options: You can bring up the three questions you've listed and apply the work of each thinker to each question, or you can explain the stances of each ethicist and show how he or she might respond to this issue. Which is best? That's up to you. Be aware that the first method might stress your issue more, and the second would probably stress the thinking of the ethicists. Either would seem to work within the boundaries of the assignment you've been given. Other organizational issues also arise. Which issue, or which ethicist, should come first? Part of effective planning is making this decision.

Looking back over the notes you have to this point, you decide to organize according to the ethicists instead of the issues. You decide to begin with France, then go to Cahill. You choose to end with Cahill because the last step of her approach will offer you a good sense of conclusion.

Now you're ready to start writing!

Some of you, though, are still staring at the computer screen. What's wrong? You're stymied by *writing the introduction.* If this is a problem for you, there are a couple of solutions. The first is to try writing the rest of the paper first and then see if you can discern how it should begin. For some folks, that method works well. For others, it does not yield results simply because their brains don't work that way. Or we may be too oriented toward moving straight through a writing, beginning to end, so that we simply can't begin without writing the introduction first. So let's take a look at how we might handle the problem of the introduction.

Writing Introductions

The good news about introductions is that you can learn one standard method that will carry you through most of your writing assignments and save you from the staring-wordlessly-at-the-monitor dilemma. Your task will be to practice the method so that when you need it, you can construct it. Like the writing process overall, creating an introduction is much more a learnable craft than a mysterious art.

If you have just one introductory style in your bag of writing tricks, the one to have is the *funnel paragraph.* This paragraph gets its name from the visual equivalent of what it does. It begins with a broad statement and then narrows down through the sentences that follow, until the central idea of the paper is expressed at the end. To construct this paragraph, we think of a broad idea about our subject and then narrow it down. The funnel paragraph is easy for writers, and it's attractive to readers in that they are led carefully to the writer's central idea. For an example, let's return to our ethics assignment. Look at the central idea: "This paper will look at the ethical issues involved in saving the lives of very premature babies." What is a more general statement on that issue? "The world is full of ethical issues"? Maybe that's a bit too big. Let's try, "New medical technologies are raising many troubling issues." That's a big statement that can lead to the central thought. Having written the broad statement, you can probably think readily of further sentences to lead the reader to your central idea. With a little experimenting, I come up with this:

New medical technologies are raising many troubling issues today. Doctors are able to save lives in ways unheard of just a few years ago. But these medical miracles do not come without cost, and today many questions emerge about who gets care and how much care is appropriate. Among the most troubling issues is the question of neo-natal care for very premature babies. This paper will look at the ethical issues involved in saving the lives of these infants.

This may not be the greatest paragraph in the world, but it will work. When I've finished the paper, I may come back and change it. But at this point I have a workable introduction.

As you read your texts and other materials, keep your eyes open and pay attention to the kinds of opening paragraphs other writers use. You will find a lot of funnel paragraphs and variations on the funnel; some writers, for example, begin with the historical background of their topic to lead to the central idea. When it's appropriate, the background paragraph is a good way to begin, because it introduces the reader to the subject helpfully. However you begin, remember that the role of the opening paragraph is twofold: It should draw the reader's attention by creating interest appropriately, and it should let the reader in on what the writing will do.

At this point, do some experimenting with the ideas set out so far. In your journal, try the rule of three with some essay assignments. First, come up with three ideas for an upcoming assignment. Choose one and then express the idea as a purpose sentence. Try posing the sentence as a question and then think of three answers to the question. Finally, work on a funnel paragraph with which you might begin the essay.

Writing Paragraphs

You have your purpose sentence in place, your introduction done, your plan in shape, and you're ready to go. Let's think now about writing those clusters of sentences that make up the large thought units of your papers: *paragraphs.*

What are paragraphs exactly? Paragraphs are units of thought, but they are also visual elements of a writing. Paragraph division can be simply an element of convenience and custom; in the past, writers commonly used much longer paragraphs than we usually employ today. Today, if you wrote a splendid ten-page paper all in one paragraph, your readers would undoubtedly be annoyed with you in spite of your excellent content, because we are used to the visual rest provided by paragraph division. Newspapers use very short paragraphs, not because their ideas aren't developed, but because the newspaper's narrow columns call for frequent visual breaks.

These issues speak to the visual aspect of paragraphing. What we will look at now is the development aspect of paragraphing. For our purposes here, we might define a paragraph as a cluster of sentences that support an idea. Often, though not always, the idea to be supported is expressed in the opening sentence of the paragraph. Sometimes one central idea binds together several paragraphs that develop that idea in varied ways. If you do not feel confident of your skills in developing paragraphs or essays, you might want to begin by creating simple, strong paragraphs that begin with sentences (called topic sentences) that set out the topic.

A topic sentence stands in relation to the paragraph as the purpose statement stands in relation to the whole essay. Look at the second point of your plan, the idea about the ethical issues regarding the suffering of very premature babies. Let's say that you have written fully about your first point, the cost involved in sustaining the lives of these babies, and now you are ready to move on. Thinking your second point through, you write, "Next we will look at the suffering of these babies," and you go on to itemize what your reading has taught you on this subject. You write a strong and effective paragraph that includes all the information and arguments you want to communicate. Essentially, your paragraph is in place, with strong content. But in rereading the beginning of the paragraph, you discover that it could be better stated. So you revise the opening sentence to read, "But it is not only the cost to the health care industry that concerns me. There is also a high cost to the babies themselves, in the terrible suffering they must endure as the hospitals labor to keep them alive."

Your new paragraph opener lacks the sharpness of the original, but it is probably better; it now includes language that moves the reader thoughtfully from one idea to the next. The original served its purpose admirably as a tool for you as a writer—it got you to focus and write with direction. But for the reader, it's possible that a smoother method will be more effective. The topic sentence is still amply clear; it's just not as stark as it was in the earlier draft.

The change in the topic sentence happened when we went through the third stage of the writing process, rewriting. Let's explore this stage further.

Rewriting

For almost all writers, rewriting (or revising) is the key to success. Like other parts of the writing process, revision is a craft we can learn. We can approach revision in stages that grow out of our individual self-understanding as writers. Some of you may be generally competent writers who rarely misspell a word or misuse a punctuation mark, but you know that your sentences tend toward sameness and that your paragraphs often lack development. Others of you may be aware that you are challenged in the area of mechanical correctness—you always have to check for syntax errors. Still others of you may feel more comfortable writing quickly without lots of planning, so you finish a draft of your essays quickly, but they often ramble or lack clear organization. All of you can make that first draft stronger by learning revision skills and applying those skills as they are relevant to your work as a writer.

Writing teachers sometimes divide revision into two kinds: global and local. What is *global revision*? As the name hints, global revision looks at the big picture created by the writing. When we do this kind of work, we ask questions like the following:

1. Does my writing do what the assignment asked?

2. Does my writing prove the point or carry out the topic as I intended?

3. Does my writing move in a clear, organized pattern, with an effective beginning and end?

4. Have I left out important points or major supporting ideas?

5. Have I wandered off my topic in distracting ways?

6. Have I created a tone appropriate to my subject and audience?

Obviously, writers who spend more time planning will spend less time on global revision. However, that does not mean that intensive planning is the best or only way to produce a draft. I know a fine writer who does almost no planning. He loves the act of writing, so he just sits and writes. To produce a ten-page paper, he will routinely write more than ten pages, hardly stopping at all. At some point, he reads what he has, and then he finds out what he wants to say: He learns what he wants to say by writing his way into it. What he ends up with is sometimes a kind of free-form writing and other times a draft, or something halfway in between. It's likely that a great deal of it will end up in the trash. He needs to do a *lot* of global revision! But this writing process works for him because he is comfortable with how he is spending his time, and because he is willing to do what he has to do to turn the "draft" into presentable and effective writing.

This method would never work for me. I like to plan carefully, and therefore I do little global revision. The key for all of us is *finding a method and committing ourselves to do the revising necessary to make that method work for us.* Unfortunately, I have had a good many students who do exactly what my friend does—just sit and write out those ten pages. But in their case, they don't revise, and they pass off the free-form writing/draft as a final version. Don't be like them!

Now let's look at *local revision.* This process involves all the things we do after we are pretty sure that an essay is satisfactory. While some of us don't do much global revision, we all need to do local revision. However, exactly *what* we do depends on us individually. Local revision can include examining these questions:

1. Are my sentences correct in terms of grammar and syntax?
2. Are my sentences strong, with varied and coherent structures?
3. Have I avoided grammar, punctuation, and usage errors?
4. Have I avoided spelling and typographical errors?
5. Is my word choice effective?

The key to effective local revision is understanding which of these questions you in particular need to address. If you get to know yourself as a writer, you will come to recognize your own strengths and weaknesses, and you'll know what weaknesses you'll probably need to correct during the local revision stage of the writing process. Some people will always wrestle with sentence correctness, and it's during local revision that they can find and correct those problems. Other people may usually write without errors, but they may have other problems. They may overuse certain sentence structures, for example, or they may make imprecise word choices. Being conscious of these tendencies, these writers can work on sentence revision and look at word choice, so that they end up with a smooth and articulate product.

What sort of revision do *you* need to do? To answer this question, think about comments you have received on your past writings. Has "frag" appeared in the margins? Have your instructors suggested that you develop your ideas more fully? Your readers, past and present, are good guides for helping you to think seriously about your revisions.

Many people primarily look at revision as a means of achieving mechanical correctness—avoiding incomplete sentences (fragments), misused commas, and other surface errors. And although real revision involves much more, revision for error correction does matter. If your professors have noted that your writing has significant mechanical problems, you need to attend to that matter—serious missteps in standard correctness, no matter how splendid your ideas, will hamper the effectiveness of your paper. The finest meal is unappetizing if it's served on a dirty plate! Let's think now about cleaning up your mechanics through local revision. How you work on this, of course, will depend on the precise tasks you identify, but here are some ideas.

First, be aware that most of us revise better with a hard copy. Some can do all their work on a computer screen, but if you discover that you fail to catch errors when you do all your revision on a monitor, you need to change your method. Print out your draft, revise the copy, and then make changes to the saved text.

Second, you need to recall what you are looking for. Do you frequently misuse commas? Then take a highlighter and dot every comma you've used, checking to see that it is correct. Do you write sentences that have structural problems? A good way to work on this error is simply to go through your draft and put brackets around each sentence. Then look at each sentence and evaluate it. You may be surprised at what you find.

Next, try reading your paper aloud. Even though your writing is likely to be intended for silent reading, you can discover a good deal about awkward spots and repetition from reading something aloud.

After doing as many of these steps as are appropriate, you will probably have made many positive changes in your writing. As you continue to make revisions both global and local, a major part of your writing process, you will discover that you gradually will do a better job in writing drafts. Of course, you may never write drafts totally free of mistakes, but you will be the only one who knows that! Most writers are quite capable of correcting many, if not all, of their own mechanical errors once they discipline themselves to go through a local revision process.

Writing Concluding Paragraphs

Many writers find that they have either an effective introduction or a good conclusion, but rarely both. You can solve this problem by thinking about what introductions are meant to do and what conclusions are meant to do, and by applying the content of your paper to both. We've already looked at how this process works with introductions; now let's think about conclusions.

First, we should realize that although all writing needs an effective ending, not all will have a genuine conclusion. You don't need to trumpet your arrival at the paper's end with a new paragraph beginning "In conclusion." Instead, think about where the content of the writing has led. What is the logical outcome of the essay? How do you want to affect your reader, and what ending will best accomplish that goal?

One classic way to end a paper is with the *look to the future* thought. Depending on the length of the essay, this "look" may be one sentence long or several paragraphs. This ending asks the reader to consider the outcomes related to your subject matter. If you have been writing about ethics, the look to the future is a sensible and obvious choice for an ending. How will the world be affected if the ethical dilemma you have described is not resolved or corrected? Or what will our lives be like if it is corrected? Your sense of your content will determine which of these you choose—you can choose to alarm your readers with the negative or reassure them with the positive. You can also choose to end your paper by explaining the *significance* of what you have discussed or argued. *Why* does this issue matter so much? *What* are the implications of your argument? Look at the big picture. Pull it all together for your reader, not in a way that insults the reader's intelligence but in a way that shows the reader connections. You can use a version of this approach by ending some papers with a look at how the subject relates to the lives of your readers. Obviously, this approach is quite relevant to many seminary projects. If you are doing a paper on Maximus the Confessor for your church history class, it is certainly a good idea for you to think about what Maximus' life has to do with ours. The end of the paper is a good place to discuss your thinking about this matter. Here are two versions of such endings, the first from a paper on the Montanist women of the early church, and the second from a paper on Saint Therese of Lisieux:

1. For the contemporary Christian reader, what is the message of the Montanist women today? Certainly their desire for self-determination in pursuing the gospel as they understood it, perhaps their desire to make Christianity more of a "woman's religion," is appealing. But many of us today are understandably nervous about the pentecostal aspect of their worship. Their contemporaries' skepticism about their fervent ecstasies instead of more common paths to the Spirit perhaps resonates with many of us. And finally, the

millennialist thrust of Montanism, though surely relevant today, would make many uncomfortable.

2. In a very different world from her own, stories of Therese's "little" life continue to be influential in some circles, where her feminine "littleness" is idealized. But perhaps it is time that *her* story of her life be read, thoughtfully and sensitively, with an eye toward resurrecting the real woman, one whose central relationships were with her sisters, one who wished she could be a priest, one who confronted a pope, and one who sacrificed all human comforts for the life of meaning that she desired. Confronting Therese in her own writings, we might find not just a saint but also a heroine.

With regard to opening paragraphs, I suggested that you think about the big issues in your subject. For closing paragraphs, you might adopt the same principle and think about the last word that you want to leave with your reader about the subject. Instead of focusing on what you can write, think about making a statement you believe in. You'll find that approach more satisfying, and so will your reader.

A Final Thought

This chapter has, I hope, given you a lot to think about and a number of new options for the writing process. What you need to do now is put some of these ideas into practice. Sometimes, inexperienced writers are challenged in trying to use what they learn; it's hard to break old habits and create new ones. Also, many inexperienced writers are not accustomed to seeing writing as a true process. They think you just pick up a pen or sit down at the computer and let the words flow—in other words, they think of the writing process as just the process of writing, letting the perfect sentences and paragraphs and pages rush out. And when the process doesn't work with such seamless perfection, they give up and think of themselves as bad writers.

I have been fortunate enough to know many professional writers, novelists, and journalists, and I've known many scholars who publish books, reviews, and articles. Of all those people,

I've known only one person for whom writing just flowed. Like those who have rare beauty or those who can eat all they want and never gain weight, she had a special gift that made life much easier for her. Having that special gift would be wonderful, but I don't have it, and you probably don't either. For the rest of us, there is the writing process. We can use it and master it and in the end come up with a product that effectively communicates our thoughts.

CHAPTER 3

Reading to Write

In this chapter, we will look at some ideas about reading. As a seminary student, you can expect to spend a great deal of your time reading: reading textbooks, of course, and also reading materials for research papers. This chapter should help you read with more efficiency and satisfaction, saving you time and helping you to avoid frustration.

Reading Textbooks

If your undergraduate major was one that did not require a lot of reading, you may at first be overwhelmed by the amount of reading expected in most seminary courses. If you are taking three or four classes, you can quickly find yourself falling behind. Then, before you know it, it's the night before the test and you have a few hundred pages to read, plus reviewing to do, *plus* a Greek quiz, *plus* a sermon to prepare, *and* a youth-group meeting…and as you look at all those pages you didn't read, you think, *There must be a better way!* And there is.

The key to managing the seminary reading load is threefold:

1. Read smart
2. Read all the time
3. Review all the time

How do you "read smart"? Reading smart simply means getting the most out of your reading time. Most of us have had the experience of reading something and forgetting it entirely within a few days, not even realizing that we've read it. If this happens with text material, we can be in big trouble! To read smart, follow several steps consistently:

First, make a practice of "prereading" your text assignments. *Much of your ability to retain material comes from the mental context you create for it.* If you pick up a book and just start reading, perhaps doing a bit of highlighting here and there, you will not remember as well as you would if you had developed some expectations about what the text might tell you. How can you do this? Before reading, look at the titles and subtitles; also, look back at what you've recently read for the class. Take a moment to think about what this chapter or section will offer you. Let's say you are reading Justo L. González's *The Story of Christianity* (vol. 2) for a church history class, and J. Christiaan Beker's *The Triumph of God* for a class in Paul. Be aware that these two readings will offer different challenges: One is fact intensive, with names, events, and dates, while the other develops ideas in subtle patterns. Central ideas will emerge quickly from skimming the first, while the second will likely require closer reading.

Be aware of the nature of the reading assignment. Look at headings and materials in boldface; these can function as road markers as you read. It's also helpful to form questions that you expect your reading to answer. Your questions might be fairly obvious: Who are the key people here? How do they differ from one another? What are the main issues or problems? You need to come away from even a quick once-over with answers to those questions. With those answers, you can go on to fill in the blanks with detail later on.

Let's say that your reading assignment for your next church history class is chapter 17, "The Puritan Revolution," in González's text. Looking at the table of contents, you note that the chapter is conveniently outlined for you, listing six names or terms, beginning with "James I" and "Charles I." Before reading the chapter, you should set the goal of finding out who these two are in relation to the Puritan Revolution. Glancing at the four remaining terms, you see "Civil War."[1] Who were the combatants in this Civil War? Where did it happen? What was at stake? What do you already know about this subject? Mulling such questions, even briefly, will help you be a wiser and more prepared reader of this chapter. You'll be reading to get answers, so what you read will be more likely to stand out in your memory. As you do the reading, create definitions of those key words. If you can say in your own words who James I was in relation to the Puritans, you'll probably be able to remember it more clearly than you would if you just highlighted key words in the text. You'll also have a better sense of what you need to know: There are a lot of names and dates in this chapter, and you need this kind of context so that you can judge what you really need to remember and what is less important supporting material.

Now, what about the Beker text? What different challenges does it offer the reader? The book's subtitle, *The Essence of Paul's Thought,* indicates the purpose of the book. A glance at the table of contents will help to set up the parameters. Looking at that page, we see that the book has a preface and is divided into two parts. Part one is labeled "The Pauline Letter" and has two chapters. Part two is "Theological Consequences" and is divided into three chapters, followed by a summary, an appendix, and a bibliography. If your assigned reading is all of part one (about thirty-four pages), you might be tempted to skip the preface. Big mistake! Don't ever skip prefaces! They tell you all kinds of helpful things about your textbooks—the evolution of the authors' thinking, issues they chose to omit, their reasons for writing, their academic or religious affiliations, the problems they encountered with the book, and the central ideas they have proposed. Sometimes they even advise the reader on how best to approach the text. Reading a preface with care is one of the best ways to create a context for understanding the text, so read it—even if it's not assigned!

---

[1]Justo L. González, *The Story of Christianity*, vol. 2 (San Francisco: Harper SanFrancisco, 1985), ix.

Reading Beker's preface, I discover that the book "posits two pillars as the foundations of Paul's thought" and then find out what those two pillars are.[2] Beker's prose style is not as easy as some, so I read this preface and try to get a sense of what his voice is like as well as what his concerns and ideas are. I find that I need to put his ideas in my own words and record those words in the margins; otherwise, I may come back to the reading and begin the same struggle of understanding all over again before long. In fact, reading the preface teaches me that I will need to do several things to get along well in Beker: First, I will need to rephrase his ideas in my own words and record them. It will also be good for me to highlight or circle his key points. In addition, I note that Beker offers headings and subheadings that, if I use them, will help to keep me focused in my reading. Finally, I realize that I need to mark and look up any words I don't know.

Building a strong theological vocabulary is an important part of your seminary education; to that end, you'll probably want to invest in a standard theological dictionary. But it is important for you to develop your general vocabulary too. If you don't already have a good desk dictionary, you should get one.[3] It will be an invaluable resource in your reading and writing. When you come across a word you don't know, you may be able to figure out its meaning from its context, but if you can't, or if you just want a more exact understanding of the word, the dictionary is at hand.

A HELPFUL TIP

If you want to retain text and lecture materials efficiently for exams, here is a tip I learned in college: Get to class a few minutes early and use the time to read through your notes from the previous period. Also, skim the reading you

---

[2] J. Christiaan Beker, *The Triumph of God: The Essence of Paul's Thought*, trans. Loren T. Stuckenbruck (Minneapolis: Fortress Press, 1990), x.

[3] Do not mistake a little paperback dictionary for a desk dictionary. Paperback dictionaries are quite limited in usefulness; you need a heftier volume. The *American Heritage* dictionaries (published by Houghton Mifflin) are excellent values, from the paperbacks to the huge ones that only libraries own. You can get a good one for $20 or so; for under $40, you can get one that includes a CD-ROM.

did to prepare for class. Then, after class, stay a minute or two and review the notes you just took. Correct any errors you see, draw lines to show connections, and highlight ideas you want to explore or now see as especially important. Most of us take notes conscientiously but don't study them until the night before the test. At that point, we're cramming the material together and simply trying to get it settled enough in our brains that we will be able to call upon it appropriately during the exam. If you use the method I have described, you will have studied all your notes *twice* even before starting to study for the exam. When you begin to study, you will be amazed at how much you remember. Furthermore, your notes will be much more useful to you because of your after-class revisions. Learning psychologists believe that we absorb more when we learn in context. Therefore, reading your notes before and after class is likely to be more powerful than sitting down with them at any other time. You read your notes; then the activities of the class reinforce what you just read. Also, what you just read helps to make the class activities more contextualized for you. Then, while all this material is still alive in your mind, you review the notes, correcting them, evaluating them, and filling them out. You have created a *learning cycle* that improves your comprehension exponentially! Try it!

Now that you know how to read smarter, you might be wondering about the second step I've recommended. How can you read *all the time*? Taking seminary classes in the midst of a busy schedule, as many of you are, I've found it helpful to carry a text with me all the time and read in bits and snatches, as I wait in the dentist's office or whatever. You will be surprised to discover how many short intervals you can find for reading, and just five or ten minutes here and there will make a big difference in what you're able to get through. (I find it helpful to write the due dates for reading assignments for the whole semester in the table of contents of each text so that I don't need to have the syllabus with me to know what I need to read for the next class.) I usually keep one text in my car and another one beside my favorite chair. By carefully using stray bits of time to nip away at reading assignments, I've found that I can then use my concentrated study time to review or work on writing assignments.

As we think of all these ways to handle the workload, we should never forget why we're doing all this. After all, scripture exhorts us to pray all the time, not read all the time, so you may find it enriching to combine steady prayer with steady reading. You may want to use a short prayer to begin every reading session, even very brief ones. "Holy God, let what I read here make me a more wise and faithful servant of the gospel" works for me.

If you do a lot of text reading in bits and pieces, you'll find it necessary to review frequently and well. The third step in effective reading is to *review all the time.* How can you do this? Let's say you are waiting for an appointment and have ten minutes or so. Picking up at the point where you ended your reading the last time, go back and look at what you underlined or highlighted. Summarize what you recall of the reading, and quickly check to see that you have the concepts or facts well in hand. This process should take only a minute or two; then you're ready to move on to further reading.

If this practice is new to you, you may be thinking that it involves too much reviewing and not enough reading. But remember that reading doesn't matter a lot unless you recall what you've read! If you read a few text pages in a noisy atmosphere, you may find your comprehension is fairly low. It's better to review and *check your comprehension* than to move ahead. I've always found that review time is time well spent. With effective and repeated reviewing of the text in this way (as well as a bit more during your concentrated study times), you will find that you already know the text well when it comes time to study for the exam. And if you have tried the method suggested above for studying class notes, you'll be in pretty good shape for any exam.

Let's turn now to another kind of reading that for some students presents a real challenge: reading scholarly articles and books in preparing a research paper. If you improve in your ability to read and work with this material, you'll do research more quickly, and you'll probably find that you are able to do more research, with more satisfaction. Some of the issues taken up here will overlap a bit with those in chapter 4, but what we want to do now is focus on doing the reading that must be done as part of research writing.

The first problem we encounter is variety. Variety may be the spice of life, but in reading scholarly material, I often find I prefer meat and potatoes to spice! The problem is this: When we read a text, we unconsciously become acclimated to the author's style, vocabulary, and organization. Thus, a two-hundred-page book is usually easier to manage than ten twenty-page articles, each of which requires us to retool our expectations. I usually feel a kind of friendship with text authors as we move through a semester; I get used to them, and I enjoy lining up my perceptions in relation to theirs or anticipating how they will approach a subject. But when I read scholarly materials in a research context, I do not have that experience. I need to switch gears with every new chapter or article and hear the voice and style of each different author. And I must decide how to use this material in my own writing. How can I do this efficiently?

The key, I've found, is again threefold:

1. Skim

2. Read selectively

3. Mark carefully

Because books and periodical articles are somewhat different in the reading styles they demand, we'll look at them separately, dealing with books and other nonperiodical resources in chapter 4. Here, we'll focus on periodicals. Let's say you're in the library and you've collected an armful of periodical volumes. (For help on how to collect those armfuls, see chapter 4.) You sit down at a desk and survey the task before you: eight volumes or so, each containing an article you may want for your paper, each article about twenty pages long–let's see–that's about 160 pages to read, and the library closes in two hours. Well, you *could* spend your two hours (and all your loose change) standing in line in front of the copier. But there is a better way.

When I'm doing research, I often find articles or books whose titles sound promising but which I discover aren't going to help me in the least. Usually I can discover this fact before sitting down with the volume. I skim the article or book when I take it off the shelf and sometimes end up putting It right back. *Skimming* is a helpful aid to research. Skimming an article or a book allows us to do a couple of things: It lets us determine the worth of a particular piece for our needs and decide how to treat it, and it lets us get a preview of the piece if we do decide to read it carefully. Again, we are building contexts for understanding.

When we skim, we are looking at headings and key words; we are also picking up a sentence here and there, which lets the author's style begin to become familiar. We are finding the range of the piece, what the author's intentions are. At this point, we know whether or not this piece of writing makes the initial cut; that is, we're sure enough that it will be useful that we take it along.

Now, back to the situation described earlier of a pile of volumes in front of you and little time in which to deal with them. At least you know that these are materials that have made the first cut. The next step is to *read selectively*. Look at an article and carefully read the opening and closing paragraphs. Look for key words and headings in the rest of the article, which would indicate that more of the article should be useful to you. At this point, you may determine that the article is important for your research and that it needs an intense and thorough reading. Set it aside for photocopying and go on to the next.

Many articles will fall in the middle ground between useless and really important. A reading of the beginning and end plus a scanning of the middle will tell you what you need to know. Try to get a quick sense of what the author is doing overall: *Don't just look for quotations for your paper.* When you have read and skimmed enough to believe you have a sense of what the article is about, look for ways the article can help you answer the questions your research topic asks. If you find long sentences and paragraphs that you think you will use, you may wish to copy them entirely so that you have the option of using them, or parts of them, as direct quotations. If you simply write down the gist of what's there, you will be able to use the thought only as an indirect quotation. And *don't forget to write down the page numbers!*

Many people today are using laptop computers to take research notes. This practice saves time and energy; you can type in your bibliographic entry right when you find the journal, then type in your notes, editing them and moving them around later on as you write. Regardless of your method of taking notes, whether you have a top-of-the-line laptop or use a pencil and pack of note cards, certain things remain the same: You need to be sure you have all the data for the bibliography, and you need to have quoted correctly, including the page numbers. I've always found that it's better to take more notes than fewer. More than once, I've copied down a few notes and later recalled a point from that article or book that would work well in my paper, only to realize that it was not in my notes. At that point I had to go back to the library and find the source again or do without the quotation–neither an option I liked! You can't always anticipate the precise direction your paper may take, so it's best to have a lot of notes to choose from. As we'll discuss in chapter 4, in research, more is always better.

Let's start to put some of these ideas to work. Below is an article from a journal you will probably use often, the *Journal of Biblical Literature* (*JBL*). Imagine that you are doing an exegesis paper for a New Testament class, and your preliminary research has led you to this article. *Skim* this article and see what information you can find. Then answer the questions that follow.

The Priest, the Levite, and the Samaritan Revisited: A Critical Note on Luke 10:31–35[4]

Why does Luke 10:29–37 contrast the intervention of the Samaritan with the refusal of the priest and the Levite to get involved? What meaning does the identity of these characters

---

[4]My thanks to Michel Gourgues, O.P., and to the *JBL* for their kind permission to reproduce this article, originally published in vol. 117 (1998): 709–13.

hold in the eyes of the evangelist? Commentaries and studies vary in their answers to these questions.[5]

Two main lines of thought tend to emerge. The *NJBC*, for example, offers an explanation typical of the first: "These leading examples of law-observant people do not aid the stripped and apparently dead man for fear of becoming defiled."[6] The difficulties raised by this explanation are well known. When Luke wants to depict a strict and rigorous observation of the law, it is not priests that he puts on stage but rather scribes and Pharisees. Thus, it is the lawyers and Pharisees who bear the brunt of Luke 11:37–53. Again, it is to them that the parable of the prodigal son is directed, representing them, so it would seem (15:2), in the figure of the elder son (15:25–32). Likewise it is a Pharisee whom the parable of Luke 18:9–14 puts in contrast with the publican. Fear of becoming defiled? It is true that contact with a corpse, according to Num 19:11–13, rendered one impure for seven days and, according to Lev 21:1–4, 11, rendered priests unfit for service in the Temple. Yet apart from the fact that the narrative reveals nothing as to their motives, it should be noted that the priest and the Levite are not on their way up to Jerusalem but on their way back. And even if the reason for the failure to intervene were to be found in the interdict posed by Leviticus 21, strictly speaking it held only for the priest and not for the Levite. Finally, the narrative provides no grounds for

---

[5]For a list of publications on Luke 10:29–37 before 1988, see F. Van Segbroeck, *The Gospel of Luke: A Cumulative Bibliography 1973–1988* (BETL 88; Leuven: Louvain University Press/Peeters, 1989) 232. Among more recent publications, see S. Légasse, *Et qui est mon prochain? Étude sur l'agapè dans le Nouveau Testament* (*LD* 136; Paris: Cerf, 1989) 67–70; K. Buason, "The Good Samaritan, Luke 10:25–37: One Text, Three Methods," in *Luke-Acts: Scandinavian Perspectives* (ed. P. Luomanen; Helsinki: Finnish Exegetical Society; Göttingen: Vandenhoeck & Ruprecht, 1991) 1–35; J. R. Donahue, "Who is My Enemy? The Parable of the Good Samaritan and the Love of Enemies," in *The Love of Enemy and Nonretaliation in the New Testament* (ed. W. M. Smartey; Louisville: Westminster John Knox, 1992) 137–56; D. E. Oakman, "Was Jesus a Peasant? Implications for Reading the Samaritan Story (Luke 10:30–35)," *BTB* 22 (1992) 117–25; J. Ziminski, "The Parable of the Good Samaritan: Asking the Correct Question," *Emmanuel* 98 (1992) 312–17; S. Légasse, "Qui est mon prochain? Réponse de l'Évangile," *Chronique* 2 (1993) 7–16.

[6]R. J. Karris, "The Gospel According to Luke," *NJBC* (1989) 702. In the same line, though more discreet, is J. A. Fitzmyer, *The Gospel According to Luke (X–XXIV)* (AB 28A; Garden City, NY: Doubleday, 1985) 887: "The implication of his passing by is to avoid contamination by contact with or proximity to a dead body."

equating the body of the beaten man with a corpse; v. 30 simply describes him as "half dead."

A second line of thought considers that Luke's mention of the priest and the Levite contains a certain anticlerical or antisacrificial barb. In fact, it would be the sacrificial regime that is represented by these characters, in opposition to the Samaritan, whom v. 37 explicitly sets forth as a witness of mercy (ἔλεος). The narrative would thus constitute a type of illustration of the oracle of the prophet Hosea (6:6): "What I want is mercy not sacrifice."[7] This line of explanation also has its difficulties. Luke, in fact, usually maintains a very respectful attitude toward the Temple and toward the priesthood. His first volume opens (Luke 1:5–25) and closes (24:53) in the Temple, and his second volume shows the disciples as faithful to regular prayers in the Temple (e.g., Acts 2:46; 3:1; 5:12, 25). It is also Luke who twice depicts Jesus as sending lepers to show themselves to the priests, thus giving further evidence of an attitude of respect toward the priesthood and the role that it fills. In Acts 6:7, Luke is proud to mention that "a large group of priests made their submission to the faith." It must also be noted that Hos 6:6, which is twice cited by Matthew (9:13; 12:7), is completely omitted by Luke.

Could one not come to some other, more satisfying, explanation, one more in keeping with Luke's vision? The following note suggests taking into consideration the social-religious order to which the narrative seems to make reference.

The Reference to a Social-Religious Order

Why a priest and a Levite? The explanation seems quite simple and in some ways completely natural if the social hierarchy of the day is taken into account. The appearance of a priest and a Levite could very well be an echo of the manner in which the different categories of the Jewish people were designated at the time.

"Priests, Levites, and all the people"; "the priests and the Levites and the people of Israel"; "the priests, the Levites, and

---

[7] Among other recent commentators who adopt this line of thought is M. D. Goulder, *Luke: A New Paradigm* (2 vols.; Sheffield: JSOT Press, 1989) 2.487.

the children of Israel": the exact formulations may vary, but ancient Judaism and the OT use this tripartite division in order to give account of the composition of religious society in its diversity.

In the OT, the formulation is found mostly in texts concerning the postexilic period. Royal institutions having disappeared, priests took on a more important role in society while the subordinate role of Levites became more clearly defined.[8] The "priest, Levite, people" trilogy figures also in certain documents from Qumran[9] and the writings of Josephus.[10] Perhaps some echoes of this division are to be found in the NT itself. Indeed, in John 1, priests and Levites (v. 19) are first sent from Jerusalem to John, after which appear the Pharisees (v. 24), which is to say, the laity.

The nomenclature is often to be found in rabbinic writings. The two following excerpts, which set Israel in contrast with the pagans, illustrate the point. The first is taken from *Gen. Rab.* 13:6.

> A gentile asked R. Joshua, saying to him, "You have your festivals and we have our festivals. When you rejoice, we do not rejoice, and when we rejoice, you do not

---

[8]The trilogy "priests, Levites, people" is to be found in one form or another in 1 Chr 28:21; 2 Chr 34:30; 35:2, 7, 18; Ezra 2:1–70; 7:7, 13; 8:15; 9:1; 10:5, 18–22, 25–43; Neh 7:72; 8:13; 10:1, 29; 11:3, 20. On Levites and the evolution in the definition of their role, see A. H. J. Gunneweg, *Leviten und Priester: Hauptlinien der Traditionsbildung und Geschichte des israelitisch-jüdischen Kultpersonals* (Gottingen: Vandenhoeck & Ruprecht, 1965); R. de Vaux, *Les institutions de l'Ancien Testament* (2 vols.; 2d ed.; Paris: Cerf, 1967) 2.257–73; M. Stern, "Aspects of Jewish Society: The Priesthood and other Classes," in *The Jewish People in the First Century* (ed. S. Safrai and M. Stern; 2 vols.; Assen/Amsterdam: Van Gorcum, 1976) 2.596–600; A. George, "Sacerdoce," *Vocabulaire de Théologie Biblique* (ed. X. Léon-Dufour; 7th ed.; Paris: Cerf, 1991) 1154–55. Curiously, the article "Levites and Priests" (by M. D. Rehm) in *ABD* 4.297–310 does not go beyond the monarchic period.

[9]E.g., 1QS 2:11, 19–21 (for the text, see *The Dead Sea Scrolls: Hebrew, Aramaic and Greek Texts with English Translations, I, Rule of the Community and Related Documents* [ed. J. H. Charlesworth; Tubingen: Mohr; Louisville: Westminster John Knox, 1994] 11); CD 14:3 (see *The Dead Sea Scrolls: Hebrew, Aramaic and Greek Texts with English Translations, II, Damascus Document, War Scrolls, and Related Documents* [ed. J. H. Charlesworth; Tubingen: Mohr; Louisville: Westminster John Knox, 1995] 57); 11QTemple, e.g., 21:4–6; 22:8–14; 57:12–15; 61:8–9 (texts in *The Temple Scroll, II, Text and Commentary* [ed. Y. Yadin; Jerusalem: Israel Exploration Society, 1983] 93, 100, 257, 278).

[10]Only in *Antiquities*, however: see, e.g., 4 §222; 7 §363; 9 §260; 11 §§74, 81, 107; 12 §142. See A. Schalit, *Namenwörterbuch zu Flavius Josephus:* Supplement I to *A Complete Concordance to Flavius Josephus* (ed. K. H. Rengstorf, Leiden: Brill, 1968) 79.

rejoice. When is it that we and you rejoice together?" [Joshua answered him,] "It is when it rains. What is the verse of Scripture that so indicates? 'The meadows are clothed with flocks' (Ps. 65:13). What occurs afterward? 'Shout to God all the earth' (Ps. 66:1) The verse does not specify priests, Levites, and Israelites, but rather 'all the earth'!"[11]

The second passage, taken from *Sifre Leviticus* 18:5 makes use of the same nomenclature at least four times.

Rabbi Meir says, "How (do we know) that even a pagan who observes (the precepts of) the Torah, must be considered the equal of the high priest? Scripture says (Lev 18:5), 'You must keep my laws and customs. Whoever complies with them will find life in them.' And (Scripture) says again (1 Sam 7:19), 'and it is the law of man.' It is not written: 'The law of *the priests, Levites and Israelites*' but 'the law of man.' Neither is it said, 'Open the gates! Let *the priests, Levites and Israelites* come in,' but (Isa 26:2): 'Open the gates! Let the upright nation come in, she, the faithful one.' Neither is it said: 'This is Lord's gateway, through which *the priests, the Levites and the Israelites,*' but (Ps 118:20), 'This is the Lord's gateway, through which the virtuous may enter.' Likewise it is not said: 'Shout for joy to the Lord *priests, Levites and Israelites,*' but, 'Shout for joy to the Lord all virtuous men' (Ps 33:1). And (neither) is it said, 'Lord be good to *priests, Levites and Israelites,*' but (Ps 125:4), 'Lord be good to the good.' From all of this one may conclude that even a pagan who follows the precepts of the Torah must be considered as equal to the high priest."[12]

These texts doubtless transmit the opinion of rabbis who lived after the first century, but it is precisely this fact that should be noted. Since the Temple and the sacrificial regime had disappeared, the tripartite division was no longer adequate to give an account of the composition of Jewish society. Thus, it cannot

---

[11]Trans. J. Neusner, *Genesis Rabbah: The Judaic Commentary to the Book of Genesis* (Atlanta: Scholars Press, 1985) 1.138 (emphasis added).

[12]This text (emphasis added) is quoted in an article by H. Krubv, which deals not with the tripartite composition of society but with the theme of neighborly love ("L'amour du prochain dans la pensée juive" *NRT* 91 [1969] 509–10).

be understood except as a remnant of an earlier state of affairs. The trilogy is already to be found in more ancient rabbinic texts, which witness to the way of thinking in Judaic circles contemporary to the origins of Christianity. Lists found in these writings always mention priests in the first place, followed by Levites and full members of Israel, the latter being distinguished from proselytes and slaves.[13]

By having first a priest and then a Levite come on stage, Luke's narrative is taking up only the first two categories from the traditional postexilic trilogy. One would then normally expect the appearance of a lay member of Israel as the third character. Thus, the surprise effect occurs when the tale substitutes a Samaritan.

In order to understand this substitution, one must bear in mind, apart from the sociological background that has just been outlined, the lawyer's question in Luke 10:29, which triggers the narration of the story: "And who is my neighbor?" The question seems to have been often debated in Judaism, especially in scribal schools.[14] The problem was to determine the implications of the precept contained in Lev 19:18, which has just been quoted in Luke 10:27, "You shall love your neighbor as yourself." Who exactly was this neighbor?

In the context of the book of Leviticus, "neighbor" (רֵעַ) included the (גֵּר) as well as Israelites, that is to say, it included the stranger who shared the land with them.[15] Scribes included this category among the proselytes[16] and were in general agreement about admitting them to the group of those covered by the injunction to neighborly love.[17] The case was different for

---

[13]J. Jeremias, *Jerusalem zur Zeit Jesu* (3d ed.; Gottingen: Vandenhoeck & Ruprecht, 1962) 304–8.

[14]Echoes of this are to be found in the sixth antithesis of Matt 5:43. For references to Judaism, see H. L. Strack and P. Billerbeck, *Kommentar zum Neuen Testament aus Talmud und Midrasch* (7th ed.; Munich: Beck, 1978) 1.353–57; for a general overview of the question, see Légasse, *Et qui est mon prochain?* 37–54.

[15]Cf. Lev 19:34: "You must count him [the stranger] as one of your own countrymen and love him as yourself." The attitude prescribed toward a stranger (גֵּר) is thus exactly the same as that prescribed in Lev 19:18b toward one's neighbor (רֵעַ), who is clearly identified as an Israelite by the titles "brother" (19:17), "neighbor" (19:11, 15, 17), "children of your people" (19: 18b) within the immediate context.

[16]The LXX had already translated גֵּר by προσήλυτος.

[17]See, e.g., *Mek. Exod.* 21:14; *Sifre Leviticus* 33:91a; cf. Stern, "Aspects," 622–24.

pure and simple non-Israelites as well as other categories of strangers, among whom Samaritans were sometimes formally classified[18]—as they are by Luke himself in 17:16–18: "...Now he was a Samaritan. Then Jesus said, 'Was no one found to return and give praise to God except this foreigner (ἀλλογενής)?'"

Had Jesus addressed the question as it existed in the mind of the lawyer, Luke's narrative would have introduced the variant on the side of the victim and not on the side of the passers-by. Love of neighbor, as it was then understood, was to be exercised toward priests, Levites, and true members of Israel, which thus excluded Samaritans. A representative of one of those categories should have taken the role of the neighbor in distress by the wayside. The narrative turns the problem on its head and situates the neighbor not among those who must be loved but among those who are to love.[19] The reversal, already implied by the parable, is made explicit by Jesus' closing question. "Who is my neighbor?" the lawyer had asked (10:29). "Who proved himself a neighbor?" now asks Jesus (10:36).

So why a priest and a Levite? Perhaps the simplest explanation is sociological in nature. The two characters whom the example story of the Good Samaritan first puts on the scene belong to the first two categories of the social hierarchy that

---

[18]See Str-B 1.354, 538.

[19]According to some authors, it is a mistake to attach undue importance to this reversal, which is thought to be purely accidental. This is the opinion of M. D. Goulder, for example: "Much discussion...has been given to the tension between 'Who is my neighbour...?' (sc. who should receive love), and 'Which of the three was neighbour ...?' (sc. who gave love). It is too subtle, however, to read theological purpose into this ...Luke's genius is in the telling of stories. He lacks a clear head to satisfy our pedantries" (*Luke: A New Paradigm*, 2.490). Others maintain that Luke held in his possession an earlier narrative that dealt with love and mercy. By inserting it artificially after the controversy of 10:25–28, he changed the point of the story by placing the emphasis not on the idea of love but on the notion of neighbor. This is what obliged him to change the perspective and situate the neighbor not on the side of the man in need but on the side of the three passers-by. Were this hypothesis to be correct, vv. 29 and 36 would be redactional elements in order to fit the story into the context. But does that change anything really? If Luke framed the story with two editorial verses, it was because he wanted the reversal of perspective. He was under no obligation to do this. Following on the preceding controversy he could very well have formulated the lawyer's question in a way that fitted with the supposed first meaning of the narrative, asking, for example, "And what does it mean to *love* one's neighbor?" To which would have corresponded a question at the end such as, "Which of the three showed that he loved?"

dominated postexilic Judaism: "The priests, the Levites, and all the people of Israel." According to this traditional tripartite division, one would expect the narrative to bring on stage next a lay Israelite. And so it is totally unexpected to see a Samaritan— a representative of one of the groups that all agreed to exclude from the category of neighbor—come on the scene and provide the answer to the question "Who is my neighbor?" (10:29).

Paradox of paradoxes, it is the Samaritan who, by means of a reversal of roles, becomes the very model of neighborly love.[20]

Michel Gourgues
Collége Dominicain de Philosophie et de Théologie, Ottawa, ON
KIR 7G3 Canada

Analysis of Reading

Now let's see what your skimming of this article revealed. Here are some points to check:

1. What question or problem is the author addressing?
2. Did you find the main idea? What is it?
3. Did you find one or two supporting ideas? Where were they?

If you have trouble answering these, review the methods for skimming and try again. If your skimming was successful, you're ready to move on.

Imagine now that you have found this article to be quite useful for your paper. You want to photocopy it (if you found it in the library) so that you can highlight and annotate it to your heart's content. I like to combine highlighting and annotation, usually highlighting the main idea and key support ideas, and numbering the key support ideas. I underline or circle important transitions such as "on the other hand" or "therefore" so that my system of marking creates a kind of physical outline for the article. In this article, for example, look at how *thus* and *so* are used to show proofs and conclusions (above, pp. 38, 39,

---

[20]I am indebted to S. Cathy McKee for the translation of this text into English.

41, 42). Notice the beginning of the second paragraph, the phrase "Two main lines of thought," followed by the quotation that Gourgues offers as summing up the first. We should be looking for the second "line of thought," and sure enough, we find it clearly placed at the beginning of the next paragraph. Gourgues has made it easy for us to follow his line of argument.[21]

Having read a significant article like this one, you will find it useful to write a brief summary of it. A few sentences, or even just some phrases, will do the trick. You might state the thesis and note the nature of the argument and its scope, as well as ways that you can connect it to other readings or to your own writing projects. This summary will serve as a comprehension check, but it will also be a good reference for the future. If you store your notes in your computer, you can search for key words later on and find this source—a bonus from your reading.

How would you summarize Gourgues' article? Give it a try—as I said, this is a good comprehension check. Think about ways you might find this article useful overall, and let that be part of your summary too. You might write something like this: "Gourgues argues that the Samaritan is especially significant not just because he is from a despised group, but because of a scriptural tradition linking priest, Levite, and then another Israelite. Extensive bibliography. Also could use for sermon on good Samaritan parable."

As you read more and more scholarly articles, you'll find that in spite of their differences, they often do have some common patterns of development. Frequently, they will begin with a problem of interpretation or an issue, then move on to discuss the standard ways of approaching the problem. Next the author will propose his or her interpretation and show why it is a good alternative or supplement to earlier ideas. Sometimes the author answers implicit or possible objections to the new idea and then concludes, often by summarizing the issue at

---

[21]Be aware that you can use Gourgues' research to extend your own. Like most authors of scholarly articles, he offers a thorough review of the relevant literature, and you can use his notes as a bibliography of sources to explore on your own.

hand, reiterating the argument, or showing the significance of the debated point. Your professor may ask you to follow this same format in writing papers; however, you can anticipate that different teachers will require different formats, depending on the nature of the assignment.

A final note: You may find some baffling spots in journal articles, primarily in the footnotes. You can respond to this by ignoring those trouble spots, and that's okay–after all, this is an essay you've chosen to read for your research, not a text. You're not obligated to know everything about it. However, if you want to get all that the essay has to give (and learn things that probably will be helpful in your further education), you can always make a note of what has stymied you and ask your professor about it. I was frustrated by reading many text references to a mysterious "LXX" before I finally learned that this was a shorthand reference to the Septuagint–an ancient translation of the Old Testament into Greek. Knowing this, I felt more initiated into the language of seminary studies. Don't be afraid to ask questions about your reading. When you do, you'll gain necessary information and greater maturity as a reader. You'll know the mysterious terms the next time you see them, and your world will be just a tiny bit bigger. That's part of what education does.

This brief chapter has certainly not covered all the issues you will encounter as you delve into seminary reading. But the principles laid out here should be of assistance to you as you deal with the basic questions of amounts and levels of reading. Remember that in this, as in most things, practice makes–well, maybe not always perfect, really. But practice does build skill and confidence levels. Happy reading!

CHAPTER 4

Seminary Research Papers

"A fifteen-page research paper is required for this course." Do those words strike fear into your heart? Many otherwise competent and secure writers feel anxiety at the idea of a research paper, and if you have not done much research writing, you may be among them. You may be wondering about all sorts of issues: What topic should I write on? How will I find the resources? How can I use the Internet? How do I cite the sources once I find them? How can I be sure I've done enough research? How do I organize such a long paper?

This chapter will build on the general writing skills discussed in chapter 2, as well as the reading skills covered in chapter 3, to navigate you through the sometimes perilous waters of research writing. We'll start with a look at the traditional place where research happens, the library.

I am very grateful to my colleague and friend Dr. Joe Pellegrino of Eastern Kentucky University, who provided much of the information on Web sites and their evaluation in this chapter.

Exploring the Library

You can count on spending a lot of time in your seminary's library, and one of the best things you can do to begin feeling comfortable with seminary research is to get to know the library long before you have to do a research paper. Exploring the library should be part of your seminary orientation, whether formal or informal. Your library probably has a number of resources available to help you get acquainted with it. Usually you will find library maps near the circulation desk. Sometimes you'll find lists of primary resources on a particular topic (for example, Native American religions, religion and literature, or bioethics). These lists, called pathfinders, offer a beginning point of research for the given topic, and examining a few of them will give you a sense of the range of the library's resources available to you on similar topics as well.

Take time to stroll around the library. You'll probably find an area that houses current periodicals; a quick glance at the titles will show you the range of materials—general interest, scholarly, and devotional—that are available to you. In other parts of the library, you'll find bound periodicals (back issues) and perhaps microform materials.

Books, of course, form the main collection of a library. Most seminaries now use a computerized system for accessing materials; these generally have a help function if you have problems in your subject search. (If the computer help is not enough, ask a real person to guide you through the process once. The computer catalog may take a bit of getting used to, but you'll find it quite easy to use before long.) Once you have a list of the books you need, you'll find them by following the shelving system in use at your library. Most shelve books by either the Union cataloging system or the Library of Congress system. In either case, you'll be able to find the books you need readily.

One of the most important parts of your library is the reference area. Browsing here will reveal a rich variety of resources, most of which you'll never need, but some of which you'll find absolutely essential. Encyclopedias and dictionaries of all sorts are housed in this area and will offer a good foundation for research. Also, in this area you will probably find the indexes that are essential for finding periodical essays on your topic.

Among indexes, *Religion Index* is the most generally helpful. If I wanted to do a paper on the religious implications of cloning, I would want a good number of periodical resources because they would be recent, so I would look up "cloning" (in alphabetical order) in the *Religion Index*. In the 1998 volume, I would discover a dozen or so entries, one of which looks like this:

Uproar over cloning. *Chr Cent* 115:76-77 Ja 28 1998.

Notice that this entry gives you all you need to make a bibliographical citation. However, the information is not presented as it would be in a bibliography. As in all writing, *purpose* governs a writer's choices. The index presents us with the title first so that we can decide if we want to pursue the article further. After the title comes the author's name, and then the periodical in which the article appears. (Note that these titles are almost always abbreviated; a list of abbreviations appears in the front of the index.) The "115" refers to volume number, "76-77" to page numbers, and "Ja 28 1998" to the particular issue. Copy this whole citation, and you'll have the information when you need it for your bibliography.

When you are researching an exegesis paper, you will want to use *New Testament Abstracts* or *Old Testament Abstracts* as well as the *Religion Index*. In addition to topic headings, each of these provides a verse-by-verse listing that will send you to those articles that comment on the passage (pericope) you're examining. However, it's a good idea to avoid confining yourself to just those articles. Instead, broaden your research and your knowledge by reading more general articles, too, acquainting yourself with the literary and social context of the passage.

Some libraries provide a reference-room guide, which will summarize the primary tools and explain which ones will be most helpful for the various research tasks you'll have. Exegesis papers obviously require different resources than papers in church history or ethics. Your professor, of course, can always provide direction in getting started.

Online Research

The field of online research is changing and growing so rapidly that any suggestions regarding methods and content would undoubtedly be outdated by the time you read them. However, certain principles do obtain. Here are some ideas to keep in mind when you enter the world of cyber-research:

- Like any other research materials, cyber-sources need to be cited. There are some special conventions regarding this kind of citation, but be aware that with this format, as with any other, the purpose of citation is to allow your reader to reach the source you used.

- Cyber-sources should be assessed carefully. Such assessment is trickier with sources garnered from the Internet than it is with periodicals or books. We assume print sources went through a jurying process, probably a highly competitive one, before acceptance, and we know that certain journals and publishers are prestigious. On the Internet, however, such is not the case. Anyone can post anything on a Web site. Looking for some fresh teaching ideas for Greek drama, I once did a search with the keyword *Antigone.* One result was a student's home page that had links to all the papers she'd ever done. Unhappily for me (and also for her!), the papers contained many factual errors and used rather poor writing style. Anyone who quoted from that paper as an authoritative source would have been in real trouble! So don't make the Internet your primary source of information, and use its resources with caution.

Evaluating Web Sites

Self-reflection is not the strong point of the World Wide Web. The appeal of the Web to most noncommercial site designers is the speed with which they can make information available to the public, not necessarily how accurate or well-designed they can make their sites. As we move from print-based reference sources to electronic sources, we should not allow ourselves to be wowed by the bells and whistles of a site; instead, we should focus on the quality of the information presented. Just as with print sources, where we check the validity of an author's claims against what other authors have written and what we already know to be true, we check the claims of a site's author against other electronic sources and authorities from other media.

The easiest and most obvious way to evaluate a site is to let someone else do it! Lycos, Magellan, Argus Associates, and other search engines routinely evaluate sites, awarding ratings based on "objective" standards. Most sites that have been given high ratings for content or structure will post such a rating prominently on their home page. This is not a guarantee of quality, but it should make you feel a bit more confident about the information you draw from that site.

For sites that haven't been evaluated already, or sites on esoteric matters that may slip under the radar of the general scholarly public, you need to apply your own critical acumen. Using the Web, you can check on the author's other works, or check on the sponsoring organization's other work. You can compare and contrast sources, read reviews, or even check newsgroups for postings on the subject.

Although there are many evaluation checklists out there, and a summary of their disparate themes is bound to be dated and noninclusive, I'll take a stab at it. Most of the checklist sites address similar topics, around issues such as these:

- Accuracy: Is the data presented factually correct?
- Authority: Is the author qualified to address this issue?
- Coverage: Does the site present the topic completely?
- Objectivity: Are there propaganda elements here? Is the author biased?
- Timeliness: How up-to-date is the information?

One of the most pressing problems of presenting accurate information about Web sites is closely related to the issue of timeliness. The Web is an ever-expanding universe, with sites coming in and out of existence at blazing speed. Consequently, any list of links is incomplete even before it is published. I have tried to avoid the 404 plague (404 is the error message your browser returns when a site cannot be found) by focusing on large, well-established pages. In general, the more inclusive a site and the larger its scope, the more likely it will be there tomorrow. Alan Liu's "Voice of the Shuttle" or The Wabash Center's "Guide to Internet Resources for Teaching and Learning in Theology and Religion" are examples of extensive sites reflecting a great deal of work, and therefore we can expect that they will be around for a while.

With all these caveats, let's move to a listing of resources. You'll find your own favorites as time goes on, but here are some to get you started. Let's begin with some sites of general interest:

http://thorplus.lib.purdue.edu/~techman/eval.html
Why We Need to Evaluate What We Find on the Internet. Adapted from *The Savvy Student's Guide to Library Research,* this page is a great outline of what you should be looking for when you look at a site.

http://www.useit.com/papers/webwriting/writing.html
How to Write for the Web. Concise, scannable, and objective. John Morkes and Jakob Nielsen weigh in with what a good site should have and how it should look.

http://discoveryschool.com/schrockguide/chaff.html
Kathy Schrock's Guide for Educators. A good starting point for analysis of a site's content quality. Her bibliography is especially helpful.

http://www2.widener.edu/Wolfgram-Memorial-Library/webeval.htm
Widener University Library–Evaluating Web Resources. This is a fine example of what's out there, with different checklists for different types of sites.

Next, let's go to some sites of particular interest for your seminary research topics. In case you are new to the electronic universe, a definition may be in order: *metasites* or *metapages* are Web sites that contain links to other sites. Here are some of the best:

http://www.academicinfo.net/religindex.html
Academic Information Subject Index: Religion. This

large metapage has links to just about everything you will need for general studies.

http://www.wabashcenter.wabash.edu/
The Wabash Center Guide to Internet Resources for Teaching and Learning in Theology and Religion. This is the most thorough guide out there for religious studies pedagogy. If you can't find it here, it probably doesn't exist.

http://www.utoronto.ca/stmikes/theobook.htm
University of Toronto–APS Guide to Resources in Theology. One of the big sites for theology, with very accurate and up-to-date links.

http://www.aarweb.org
The American Academy of Religion. *The* scholarly group for theological studies.

http://davidwiley.com/religion.html
Marshall University–Sacred and Religious Texts. You'll find a great collection of links to electronic versions of sacred texts here.

http://www.acs.ucalgary.ca/~lipton/biblio.html
University of Calgary–Bibliographies on the Web. An excellent collection of secondary source materials.

http://www.fontbonne.edu/libserv/fgic/contents.htm
Fontbonne College–Finding God in Cyberspace. A good guide to religious studies resources on the Internet.

http://vos.ucsb.edu/shuttle/religion.html
University of California, Santa Barbara–The Voice of the Shuttle. Alan Liu's work is outstanding for its breadth.

If you are looking for church history or ecclesiology materials, here are some possibilities:

http://cedar.evansville.edu/~ecoleweb/
University of Evansville–The ECOLE Project. An encyclopedia of early church history. Very impressive, especially the chronology/geography timeline.

http://netserf.cua.edu/religion/default.cfm
Catholic University of America–Netserf–Medieval

Religion. A very thorough site on church history of the Middle Ages.

http://www.sc.edu/ltantsoc/
University of South Carolina–Society for Late Antiquity. An excellent specialized site, listing plenty of resources for ecclesiology in this period.

http://www.definingmoment.com/ric/refrigerium/
Refrigerium Early Christian Web Site. A good collection of patristic writings here.

For biblical studies, try these:

http://www.biblelearning.org/
The Bible Learning Center. A searchable site, sometimes a bit simplistic, but a good starting point for research.

http://www.christianity.net/bible/
Christianity Online–Bible and Reference. An excellent site with plenty of pastoral information.

http://www.aril.org/Bible.html
ARIL–Biblical Resources. Another great metasite with award winners from ARIL.

http://bible.gospelcom.net/bible
The Bible Gateway. Full searchable texts of eight different translations.

http://www.religioustolerance.org/chr_cs.htm
ReligiousTolerance.org–Christian Scriptures (New Testament). A good site, especially the "Descriptions of Individual Books of the Christian Scriptures" section.

For research on ecumenism and world religions, look at these resources:

http://www.eni.ch/latest.html
Ecumenical New International. This includes daily updates on issues and stories concerning ecumenism.

http://www.wcc-coe.org/
The World Council of Churches. Includes 336 churches of almost all Christian denominations in 126 countries.

http://www.aril.org/World.html
World Religion Resources. A great metasite where every linked site has received the ARIL Hot Site designation as offering among the best resources concerning world religion on the Internet.

http://www.religioustolerance.org/
Ontario Consultants on Religious Tolerance. An impressive multicultural look at religious experiences throughout the world.

If you are doing research in the area of homiletics, go to these sites:

http://www.wabashcenter.wabash.edu/Internet/
preach.htm
Wabash Center Internet Guide–Preaching. An eclectic collection of sites and other resources. You may be overwhelmed by the amount of information here.

http://divinity.lib.vanderbilt.edu/homiletics.htm
Vanderbilt University–Homiletics in the Divinity Library. An excellent resource, both scholarly and practical.

http://www.mumac.org/ppcss.html
Pastor's Pointers Christian Sermon, Worship, and Bible Site. A huge list of individual sermon sites. As with any site of this nature, the quality varies, but the selection is good.

http://www-oslo.op.org/library/mpreach.htm
Dominican Web Library–The Ministry of Preaching. Fr. Damian Byrne, O.P., the Master of the Order of Preachers, addresses the topic.

http://homileticsonline.com/default.asp
Homiletics Online. You need to subscribe for full access to this site, but you can read the cover story and the back page for free.

http://www.montreal.anglican.org/comment/
Commentaries on the Revised Common Lectionary. A very good site in the Anglican tradition.

http://www.vsg.cape.com/~dougshow/second-site/index.html
The Exchange for Sermon and Worship Ideas. An interesting site, a sharing of resources for working preachers.

Finally, when your research needs are in the area of ethics, try these resources:

http://ethics.acusd.edu/kant.html
University of San Diego–Ethics Updates. This site is one of the most comprehensive, with sections on ethical theory and applied ethics, as well as links to many other sources.

http://www.depaul.edu/ethics/resource.html
DePaul University–Ethics Resources on the Net. This metasite has a good sampling of links, but its strength lies in its categorization of ethical studies.

http://www.depaul.edu:80/ethics/
DePaul University–Institute for Business and Professional Ethics. The mother site of the previous link, this is a good overview of business and professional ethics.

http://www.lcl.cmu.edu/CAAE/80130/syllabus.html
Carnegie Mellon University–Introduction to Ethics Course. Although parts of this site are password-protected, what remains in the public domain is a very good introduction to ethics.

http://condor.depaul.edu:80/ethics/ethg1.html
DePaul University–The On-Line Journal of Ethics. A very good Web-only resource with interesting, timely articles.

http://www.ethics.ubc.ca/resources/
University of British Columbia, Centre for Applied Ethics–Resources for Applied Ethics. Another metasite with great resources for applied ethics.

http://www.ethics.org/
Ethics Resource Center. An interesting organization. Not

a lot of information here, but the results of their business ethics surveys are thought provoking.

http://www.utm.edu/research/iep/
University of Tennessee at Martin–The Internet Encyclopedia of Philosophy. Accurate short articles on various philosophers and issues in philosophy. Articles on individual philosophers usually address their ethical stances.

http://astro.temple.edu/~dialogue/geth.htm
The Center for Global Ethics. This site coordinates the work of thinkers, scholars, and activists from around the world who are working to define, implement, and promote policies of responsible global citizenship.

Choosing Topics and Using Research Resources

Now that we have a good idea of what resources are available for research, let's step back and look at what else we need to know. What is "research writing" about? How does it differ from other writing assignments? What special concerns does it present?

In the preceding chapter, we looked at ways to find topics and examine them for appropriateness. These issues become all the more important when we approach research writing. It's hard to come up with a research topic early in the semester, when you don't have a full sense of all that the course will offer. One practical bit of advice is to *talk with your professor* about topics. In some classes, of course, you'll be given a list of choices, but in others the field is open. If the professor simply asks for a fifteen-page paper on something in early church history, you may well want more guidance. A poor topic choice may leave you with a subject that will be difficult to research, perhaps because the topic is too broad or even too narrow. The professor is your best resource to guide you in an effective topic search.

Once you have an appropriate topic, you will find it helpful to *frame the topic as a question that your research will answer.* You may have a cluster of questions, but try to think in terms of one centering question. This kind of focus will lend meaning to your research and unity to your paper. I once decided that I would write a research paper "on" Saint Therese of Lisieux. I knew almost nothing about her. A quick glance through the library revealed lots of resources. Where was I to start? Was I to read all the books and articles about her? My problem was that I did not know what I was looking for. It's pretty hard to find something when you don't know what you're looking for! So I scanned some general articles about her and decided to narrow my focus to her autobiography, *The Story of a Soul.* I also learned that two twentieth-century women, Vita Sackville-West and Dorothy Day, had written biographies of Therese. I decided that I would read the biographies and compare them with the autobiography. I wanted to know what these modern women saw in Therese and how they understood her life as compared with how Therese understood herself. Noticing that there were a good number of current articles about her, as well as a film, I wanted to know what contemporaries saw in her too.

My preliminary research had led me to want to know these things, and that's always a good beginning for a research project. If you're going to spend a significant amount of time on a subject, it helps if you have genuine questions and can take pleasure in discovering their answers.

Now that we know something more of what we're looking for, it's time for a more focused trip to the library and to the Internet. Let me offer some practical pointers. They may seem overly obvious, but at some point we all waste time by missing the obvious.

- Take the supplies you will need: your library card, change for photocopying, pens, note cards (if you prefer taking notes with them), and your course syllabus or other information you've been given about the assignment. You might also take along a snack and a few aspirins!

- Keep records of what you've done. If you do periodical research today and don't get back to look at books for a while, you may forget what terrain you've already covered. Write yourself a note about what indexes and other resources you've used.

- Write down (or print out) *all* bibliographic information when you use a source. If you are not clear on what information is required, find out, or take the appropriate style manual with you to the library. It may seem like a pain, but it's not nearly as bad as the jolt you get when, at midnight the night before the paper is due, you realize that you did not write down the city of publication for any of the books you used. Today, of course, with so many materials available online, many of us can access our library's catalog from home to get the missing data. But don't count on that. Just do it right the first time!

Constructing the Research Paper

So you've been to the library and visited Internet sites. You have a number of sources—some well-chosen, current periodicals, some Internet documents perhaps, and some books. You sit down with a pile of note cards, photocopied articles, and computer printouts. You think there is ample research here. But what next? How do you turn all this stuff into an articulate essay?

At this point, you need to withdraw from your research a bit. Set it aside and go back to where you were when you began this project. What was your initial question? Have you found answers to it? Did your research take you in a new direction? What are the main things you've learned from your reading? What are the main things your reader should learn from this paper?

Once again, it is good to review the precise assignment you were given. Seminary papers often have explicit divisions that you need to use. An exegesis paper, for example, may have an "application" section at the end. If your professor has asked for a specific structure, use it! Often that structure will be extremely helpful to you, essentially organizing the paper for you. For example, a church history assignment I was once given asked students to select a significant person discussed in our text and further explore that person's life and writings, describing the person's historical context, explaining his or her theology, and relating the theology to the context. We were to conclude with a personal response to the person's work. Planning such a paper was an easy task because an orderly four-part structure had been offered.

But if we need to come up with our own structures, what then? Where do we start? Well, go back to chapter 2 and review if you need to, because what you need to remember at this point is that *organizing a research paper is like organizing any other paper*. We often get so concerned about the research angle that we forget this basic fact. *We* are the constructors of knowledge when we write. We need to recall that the research is a tool to develop our own ideas. When we do research, we are not just passive recipients of information. As we read, we should always be measuring what we're reading against what we already know. We should be thinking, comparing, wondering, challenging. As I do research, I take notes on my reading, not just recording the content of an article but noting how I can use a quotation I've just written down. I have a habit of making my own comments in brackets so that I can see clearly what the author's thought is and what mine is. If you looked at my notes, you'd find bracketed comments like these: [use for conclusion?] [Baker disagrees with this interpretation!] [I can add some arguments here]. All of these will help me when it's time to write.

And now it is that time, almost. I've got plenty of material and a rough plan for my paper, and looking at my plan, I'm pretty sure that the paper will be about as long as it should be. But before I begin to write, it's good to put all my notes in some sort of order. I find it helpful to label the points of my plan alphabetically, then label my notes according to where in the paper I intend to use each one. (If I have a lot of highlighters around, I'll use them and color-code my plan points and notes.) Obviously, the more complete my plan is, the easier it will be to label the notes accordingly. If you take notes on a laptop, you may find it worthwhile to print them out in order to do this step of the process. A benefit of this approach is that, seeing your notes stacked up against your plan, you can tell whether or not you do in fact have ample sources. Of course, it's not necessary that each part of your essay cite the same number of sources, but if you discover that one section is significantly low on research and would profit from more, you may want to make one more trip to the library.

As you plan and write, be aware that many research papers are seriously flawed because the writer has failed to use sources well. If you are inexperienced in writing research papers, you may be tempted to make your essay into a simple summary of your research. So you write a paragraph in which you summarize everything you learned from source A, then a second paragraph telling what source B had to say, and so on. This series of mini–book reports does not constitute an effective research essay! It does not show you, the writer, thinking through the issues. Remember that you need to *construct a line of argument,* effectively marshaling the research to carry out the argument. I have sometimes read research papers in which any paragraph could be interchanged with any other paragraph: The student was simply offering a cluster of summaries and randomly chosen quotations that had some vague bearing on the topic. Don't fall into this trap. Making a plan and using sources to build paragraphs that carry out the plan will create a genuine essay.

The actual writing of your essay should not be too difficult now that you have taken the steps laid out above. Use the tools discussed in chapter 2 to come up with effective opening and closing paragraphs, and your first draft is done. Now it's time to work on *revising the research paper.* General revising skills are discussed in chapter 2, and all of them should come into play here. But when you are writing a research paper, you need to use special revising skills as you look at sentences within paragraphs. What are these special concerns? First, you want to be sure that you have indeed organized your paper appropriately (see the global revision discussion in chapter 2). Have you avoided the "book report" format? Of course, from time to time there may be a good reason to use one source extensively in one section or paragraph of your essay. But be sure you are doing so because the content demands it and not because you have fallen into the book report mode.

Next, you want to check to see that you have *used your sources and quotations appropriately and smoothly.* Using quotations well is one of the biggest challenges for the writer of research papers. As you become more experienced in research writing, you'll find these choices easier to make. Here are some general rules:

- One of your goals should be to get more of your own thoughts into the paper. Think about your subject matter and about your completed research. Do you agree with all that you've read? Compare what different scholars have said and comment on the similarities or differences. What have the scholars omitted or avoided? Draw hypotheses, or at least note what's not there. Create a synthesis as a topic sentence for some paragraphs. If you are doing an exegesis paper on a biblical passage and you discover that scholars have written lots on verse 16 but little on verse 17, you might begin the paragraph discussing verse 17 with something like this: *Relatively few scholars have commented on verse 17.* Perhaps you've found that scholars disagree sharply on the meaning of verse 16. Saying so will create a good topic sentence for the paragraph in which you recount their findings. Such sentences will not need footnotes because they come from your observations on the materials you've found.

- Often students make research harder for themselves than it should be because they look only for sources that will answer their questions or speak to their issues head on. Be aware that the broader your research, the better. Let's say you are doing a paper for an educational ministry class, and your topic is educational ministry with Hispanic teens. That's a pretty narrow topic, and you may not find a whole lot of material speaking directly to the subject. However, you can find all the material you want on teen ministry overall, and lots on ministry in the Hispanic community. Use your experience and intelligence to put the two together. In this way, you are adding to knowledge, not just compiling it.

- As you do research, copy direct quotations. As you write the essay, you can choose to make them into indirect quotations. You can go from direct to indirect, but you can't reverse the process without a trip back to the source.

- Using a *long* direct quotation involves some format rules. Different style manuals mandate different specifics; you need to find out what yours requires. Some say that a quotation running more than four typed lines should be double-indented and single-spaced. Such a quotation is usually introduced with a colon.

- You should minimize use of long direct quotations. Like the mini–book report style, a lot of long quotations can make your paper seem like a series of undigested gobbets of other people's thoughts on your subject. If you are concerned that you have this problem, your revising process should include printing out your paper and highlighting every direct quotation. If your paper is more highlighting than anything else, do some revising.

- If you have converted direct quotations into indirect ones, you should clarify where quotations begin and end. If you begin a paragraph with a terrific idea of your own and then follow with an indirect quotation from Smith, you want to make it clear that Smith doesn't get credit for your great idea. Solve this problem with introductory tags to let the reader know where Smith's thought begins. Some common tags are these: *Smith contends, Smith argues, as Smith says, Smith believes,* and *Smith concludes.* Follow this tag with your indirect quotation and conclude it with a footnote or parenthetical note. The tag and the note function as quotation marks would to set off Smith's thought and clarify what is Smith's and what is yours or someone else's.

- Does your paper have too many footnotes, cluttered with lots of *ibid.*'s? You can often solve this problem by combining several footnotes into one. (Check with your professor about this practice, as he or she may prefer the more detailed notes.) If you begin a paper with biographical information, indirectly quoted and all from one source, you can put just one footnote at the end of the material. The footnote would read something like this: "This biographical material is summarized from M. A. Robinson, *Bid the Vassal Soar* (Washington, D.C.: Howard University Press, 1974), 14–36."

- It's important to integrate direct quotations into sentences. Rarely, if ever, should a direct quotation stand on its own as a sentence. If you want to quote a full sentence, don't let it stand alone; rather, introduce it by connecting it to the preceding sentence with a colon. If it doesn't sound right that way, you need to find a better sentence to introduce it. Your goal, after all, is to have a coherent, organized flow of thought. A paragraph full of random, orphaned quotations is not what you want. As you think about and understand your sources, you will discern ways to use direct quotations more smoothly.

- Remember that you are responsible to the author to quote correctly and to give credit. However, you are not required to quote a full sentence just because you copied it down. Here's an example from a paper on African American religious poet Phillis Wheatley. The quotation I've written down is this: *Born in Africa and brought as a slave to America before the Revolution, Phillis Wheatley learned to write like a European. But this is not to say that she wrote as a European, nor is it to say that she did not.* I want this idea in my paper, but since I've already covered Wheatley's background, the first part of the sentence is irrelevant and would simply distract the reader. Instead, I take the heart of the quotation, the memorable words, and create a more pithy sentence, combining direct and indirect quotation: *Silvers believes that, while Wheatley "learned to write like a European," she did not necessarily write "as a European."*[1]

You also need to be sure that you avoid plagiarism. Of the most egregious kind of plagiarism, the conscious stealing of whole essays or passages, nothing need be said. But there are more subtle forms. Plagiarism can occur when you paraphrase a source and do not clearly cite it. The key to avoiding unintentional plagiarism lies in being careful—that is, full of care and respect for the researchers whose work is underpinning your own. If you have that attitude of care, you will record your sources completely as you do research, make your citations clear to give credit where it's due, and take the time to

[1]Anita Silvers, "Pure Historicism and the Heritage of Hero(in)es: Who Grows in Phillis Wheatley's Garden?" *Journal of Aesthetics and Art Criticism* 51 (1993): 476.

understand your sources and therefore be able to express their thoughts *in your own words* when you choose indirect quotations.

Using Citation Styles

Your research paper should use a consistent citation style. As an undergraduate, you probably used MLA style (used commonly in humanities disciplines), APA style (used in social and behavioral sciences), or the University of Chicago Press style (also called "Turabian" after Kate Turabian, author of an abbreviated manual of Chicago style). Your seminary or your professor may have a preferred or mandated style. You need to find out what style is required, get the appropriate style manual, and use it.

If you are used to one style and have to change to another, you may find the change disruptive. However, you should know that certain principles underlie all styles. For books, you will always need to cite author, title, city of publication, publisher, and year of publication. If you have all these items in your bibliography, you may still make some small errors but not the big ones! Remember that your goal is to be accountable and responsible, giving credit where it's due and also giving your reader information so that he or she may locate the source. Two of the most common styles, MLA and Chicago (Turabian), are represented in the sample research papers at the end of this chapter.

Formatting Your Paper

There are few one-size-fits-all rules for format. Some teachers prefer a separate title page, while some prefer title page information in an upper corner on the first page. Some style manuals give standards for formatting papers (see part 1 of Turabian's manual, for example, or chapter 3 of the *MLA Handbook*). Some common standards, however, will always give your paper a professional appearance:

- Whether it appears on the first page or on a title page, center your title and *don't* put quotation marks around it.

- Use a traditional font such as Times New Roman or Courier—no cursive or fancy ones, attractive as they may be.

- Use a twelve-point font and standard margins. Don't use the "loaves and fishes" method of trying to make an eight-page paper look like the twelve pages the professor asked for by expanding the text with oversized margins and big fonts! Nor should you test your professor's eyesight by reducing the font size of an over-long paper. Instead, use judicious editing to shorten the paper.

- At the end of the text of your paper, move to a new page to begin your endnotes, if you have them, and then move to another new page for your bibliography.

A Final Reminder

We may take it as evidence of the fallen nature of humankind that we so often, in spite of our best resolves, wait until the last minute to finish these major projects. Then, of course, we are prey to all the ills that seem to afflict the rushed project—the computer loses text, the printer fails to print, you name it. As a result, we often find ourselves completing a major project at the very last minute, with no time to do any level of revision. I hope that chapter 2 persuaded you that you need to revise. And nowhere is that need greater than in a research paper. Effective use of quotations comes, for many of us, not in our writing but in our revising. Other elements of global revision will be necessary more in the research paper than in other writing assignments. And, of course, we always need to save time for local revision. It does not speak well of our seriousness as students if we turn in a term paper, a paper that was to be the term's project, without having proofread it adequately. Give this last stage of the process its due, and don't undercut your effectiveness as a writer by letting sloppy work go out under your good name!

Sample Paper in MLA Style:
Luke 10:38–42: Exegesis and Criticism

While they were on their way Jesus came to a village where a woman named Martha made him welcome

in her home. She had a sister, Mary, who seated
herself at the Lord's feet and stayed there listening to
his words. Now Martha was distracted by her many
tasks, so she came to him and said, "Lord, do you not
care that my sister has left me to get on with the work
by myself? Tell her to come and lend a hand." But the
Lord answered, "Martha, Martha, you are fretting and
fussing about many things; but one thing is necessary. The part that Mary has chosen is best; and it
shall not be taken away from her." (Luke 10.38–42,
NEB)

This brief, typically Lukan pericope has engendered a vast
amount of critical attention. A narrative and pronouncement
story, the passage defies easy explication because of the ambi-
guities, both textual and interpretive, of the pronouncement
itself. In theology, spirituality, and church history, the Martha-
Mary story has become a rich source of discussion. This essay
will look at the context (both within Luke and within the Gospels)
and form of the pericope and its three main lines of
interpretation. The essay will also include some synthesis and
commentary.

The most traditional way of interpreting the Martha-Mary
text is to read it as a discussion of the tensions between the
active life and the contemplative life. In this reading, Martha
represents the doers of the world, while Mary represents those
who meditate or learn. Jesus's clear approval of Mary's path, it
has been argued, is a statement in favor of the superiority of
the life of the mind or spirit. Peter Erb summarizes this argument effectively (163–64) and, furthermore, ties Jesus's approval
of Mary to the preceding parable, arguing that the two together
illustrate the two great commandments: the Samaritan illustrates love of one's fellow humans, while the Martha-Mary section illustrates the love of God (163).

Erb is not alone in the specifics of his interpretation. Frederick
W. Danker, for example, suggests that the Martha-Mary story
"does not pit passivity against action, but motivates activity
with receptivity to the Benefactor's word. Martha reflects another phase of the self-righteous legalist; Mary is the potential
Good Samaritan" (94). David Lawton believes that the pericope

is a contrasting "corrective" to the Good Samaritan parable (50), which has perhaps emphasized action too much; Dennis Sweetland states that the Good Samaritan is "balanced" by the Martha-Mary account (330). G. H. P. Thompson reads the text in much the same way, finding interest in the fact that the "practical Samaritan" is approved, while the practical Martha is "rebuked" (167–68). O. C. Edwards (57) and Craig A. Evans (177) accept this reading, while Norval Geldenhuys (316) modifies it somewhat, contending that the point is that the active life must not be a "sulky and dissatisfied one." An audience-appropriate note is sounded by E. Earle Ellis, who claims that the "issue is not two kinds of Christian service but the religious busyness which distracts the Christian—preacher or layman —from the word of Christ upon which all effective service rests" (160).

An argument from form as well as content comes from Charles H. Talbert (120), who like Erb sees the commandments connection and who contends, as Erb does (163), that the "chiastic pattern" used commonly by Luke makes the two pericopes in fact one (125). Joseph A. Fitzmyer, on the other hand, finds the love of God/love of neighbor connection unconvincing (891).

Less has been said about the connection of the Martha-Mary story to the account that follows it, the teaching on how to pray. Mary Rose D'Angelo notes that the teaching on prayer is specifically represented in Luke as a teaching on proper discipleship, a view which would relate the two (455). This reading seems to emphasize a tenuous connection, relying almost solely on the articulated occasion ("Lord, teach us to pray as John taught his disciples") for the giving of the prayer rather than on the prayer itself.

A second major trend in interpreting this pericope is to see it as one that validates the right of women to discipleship and to "solid theological education" (Schaberg 289). Thomas Bernhard views the passage as affirming the right of Catholic women to the priesthood today (263). Constance Parvey sees the pericope as affirming one woman's, and by extension all women's, right to choose to learn (141). How new this choice was in the days of Jesus is disputed: Schaberg points out that in fact there was no actual prohibition against women's studying the Law (288); however, it is likely that "no real rabbi would teach a woman," as Eduard Schweizer notes (189). Therefore, Jesus's affirmation of Mary has revolutionary intent. As Richard J. Cassidy argues, one may see Jesus as adopting "a pattern of behavior that implicitly opened the way to new personal and social standing for women" (37).

While these arguments focus on the affirmation of Mary's role, other scholars choose to stress the comparison of the two sisters, to Martha's detriment. In fact, support for Mary's "part" of discipleship has led to a degree of what might be termed "Martha-bashing." While Jesus does not in any sense condemn Martha, the same cannot be said for many scholars. Danker, as has been seen, views Martha negatively as a "legalist" (84). And I. Howard Marshall, to cite another example, contends that Martha's busyness was shown as a lesson to the women of Luke's church, illustrating how *not* to entertain visiting missionaries (451). Jane Kopas, who is more sympathetic to Martha, believes that her actions are acceptable but her attitudes need adjusting (198). Geldenhuys's reading is similar; he contends that the active life Martha has chosen must not be "anxious, and agitated, sulky and dissatisfied" (316). But John Paul Pritchard, a severe critic of Martha, sees her as "fussy" (123) and "petulant" (196) in the Lukan narrative and "confused" (197) in John 10.21–27—a rather unjustified characterization in light of Martha's strong, twofold confession of faith in this passage.

The reading-into of the text's *perispao* (a word that appears only on this one occasion in the New Testament) seems a bit unfair, even if coupled with Martha's request/plaint to Jesus. A different and more positive focus comes if one looks at Martha's situation and her precise words: what the New English Bible renders as "lend a hand" is the Greek *synantilabetai,* literally, "to take hold with at the side" (J. D. Douglas 250). The word is used only here and in Romans 8.26, in the very powerful passage on the Holy Spirit who "comes to the aid of our weakness." The use of this unusual word may suggest that Martha is not a whiner or spoilsport but rather someone who, being troubled about many things, feels the need of the support and companionship of her sister.

Although the Martha-Mary story is unique to Luke, an understanding of this passage may be enhanced by a comparison with the appearances of Martha and Mary in John's gospel, 11.45 and 12.1–8. To see such a relationship between the two accounts is not inappropriate: Marshall believes that Luke probably knew the tradition of Mary and Martha stories from John's gospel (451); Fitzmyer is less sure, suggesting that Luke's own source is the most relevant one, but "contact with the developing Johannine tradition is not impossible" (891). Prichard, on the other hand, sees the line of influence as going from Luke to John, with John's version of Martha and Mary growing from other traditions, too, now lost to us (196).

A comparison of the two Gospel accounts is instructive. First, in regard to the status of Mary, it is interesting to note that although Martha is apparently the one who owns the home (Luke 10.38), it is Mary who seems to have more public stature. When their brother Lazarus has died, the Jews come to mourn with both women (John 11.19), but further reference has them "condoling with Mary" (11.31) and visiting with Mary (11.45) at the time when Lazarus's raising occurs.

Furthermore, during the supper described in John 12, Martha is again serving, in the same sense described in Luke, while Mary is again at the Lord's feet. Each time Mary appears, she is in this position: when she and Martha meet Jesus after Lazarus's death, but before his raising, Mary falls at Jesus's feet, while Martha does not. Both women seemingly reproach Jesus with the same sentence ("If you had been here, my brother would not have died"), but Martha goes on to express faith in Jesus, first by saying "Even now, I know that whatever you ask of God, God will grant you" (11.22) and then by responding to Jesus's self-revelation by an echo of Peter's recognition (Mark 8.29) of Jesus's Messiahship: "I now believe that you are the Messiah, the Son of God who was to come into the world" (John 11.27). It is interesting that while scholars traditionally have read Mary as the "real" disciple and Martha as the one given the lesser part, it is Martha who recognizes Jesus' Messiahship and his nearness to God—and recognizes this even before the raising of Lazarus.

Mary, on the other hand, is always presented at the feet of Jesus in the Lukan and in the Johannine accounts. She falls at his feet when she meets him after her brother's death; she is at his feet hearing his teachings in Luke's account. In John 12, she anoints his feet with perfume and wipes them with her hair, an interesting reversal of the common custom of anointing a guest's head with oils. Her abject humility and reverence for the Lord are the outstanding characteristics that appear in this action. It is only a few days later that Jesus, at supper, washes the feet of his disciples. Though the action was a common one in the ancient world, the juxtaposition of the two accounts in John's Gospel has the effect of making Mary's action a forerunner of Jesus's, her gesture of total service and self-abnegation contextualizing his. That the washing of the disciples' feet in John takes the place of the institution of Eucharist in the synoptic Gospels intensifies this relationship. Martha "serves" the Lord in one important sense, at the table, but Mary serves in another way. As Schaberg notes, *diakonia* of the table and of the word are integrated in John's Gospel, and the two women do not appear in conflict (289). It is Judas who introduces the note of discord here, telling the Lord that the oil should have been sold for the poor. Jesus's response is in essence the same as it was to Martha in Luke's account: Mary should be left alone to do what she is doing.

A third major way of reading the pericope, and the most contemporary, is one voiced most powerfully by Elisabeth Schüssler Fiorenza, who argues that the text is in fact *not* intended as an affirming one for female ministry or discipleship. Rather, she maintains that the passage specifically disempowers women by limiting their "ministry" to listening, not doing. Schüssler Fiorenza sees Luke as advocating a division of *diakonia*, service into those roles assigned to men and to women (32). In a carefully drawn argument, she concludes that the story of Martha and Mary functions "as prescriptive rhetoric in the historical situation of women's struggle against the gradual patriachalization of the church at the turn of the first century" (33). While Fiorenza's argument is focused toward an understanding of the evolution of church practice, other contemporary commentators have looked at the pericope with a slightly different focus but a similarly skeptical eye. Schaberg (288–89) makes much of Mary's position at the Lord's feet, contrasting her with the apostles, who listen to the Lord, but who are not described as being in a position of subservience (289). Similarly, Gail Patterson Corrington argues that a woman's discipleship in Luke "seems mainly to be of the passive, receptive variety" (162).

We may, if we wish, read this passage as a seriously anti-feminist, or even anti-female, text. Schaberg (288–89) notes that the sisters never speak to each other. Indeed, one might say that Jesus is used as the intermediary, the alpha male whom Martha desires to use to call Mary back to her appropriate role. That Jesus allows Mary her position as a disciple has made this text seem a hopeful one for women in ministry, though perhaps a negative one for women with a need of household help. But Schaberg's conclusion is exactly the opposite. She emphasizes the passivity of Mary's "discipleship": Mary never answers the Lord in Luke's account, never asks questions as the "real" apostles do, and is a quintessential follower. Shaberg flatly says that it is "Luke's intent…to undermine the leadership of women" (289). Martha, the active party who owns the house, confronts the Lord, and in general *acts* in the world, is the one who is reproached.

But there are more positive ways of reading this pericope. If we begin with Jesus's pronouncement, to which the narrative obviously leads, we may see the text as one of potential reconciliation between the sisters rather than one in which Jesus simply picks the better sister and announces his choice to the loser. Traditionally, our reading of this and most other parables and narratives has tended toward dichotomy: the rich and the poor, the just and the unjust, the Good Samaritan and the bad Jews, Lazarus and Dives. However, a more positive reading is possible, one in which both Mary and Martha are affirmed. Although its position has made the Good Samaritan parable the one often paralleled to the Martha-Mary pericope, perhaps an equally instructive comparison is to the story of the Prodigal Son. It is not difficult to see Jesus's part as analogous to that of the father in the parable; thus, in both cases we see siblings in conflict, one doing the usual thing and one not. In both cases the father (or father figure, Jesus) intercedes to comfort the one who has done the usual thing and feels overlooked. Perhaps most importantly, both tales end, intentionally or unintentionally, with lacunae. The reader does not know if the elder brother will accept his brother's return and his father's joy and therefore join the banquet. Nor is Martha's response to Jesus given.

She is troubled about "many things," as the Lord sees, so it seems clear that kitchen help is not the sole issue. We may read both pericopes as possessing hopeful endings in the healing and loving words of the father/Jesus.

The pronouncement itself has four distinct portions. First, Jesus tells Martha something significant about herself: "Martha, Martha, you are fretting and fussing about so many things." Next, he makes a general statement: "but one thing is necessary." Third, he evaluates Mary's action: "The part that Mary has chosen is best," and finally, he tells what will be: "and it shall not be taken away from her." The second of these pronouncements is usually seen as the one most open to interpretation (what *is* the "one thing" that is necessary?), but a careful look at the whole pronouncement may yield a helpful conclusion.

The first and second segments are interdependent in their interpretation. There are two senses of what these lines may be saying, one literal and one figurative. First, they may be read as Jesus's helping Martha to understand that she is upset about more than she knows. There is an apt point to be made about human relations here (how often are our fights with family members really about the surface issues, and how often are we in fact "troubled about many things"?) that may have homiletic potential. A second interpretation is simpler, that the "so many things" refers to Martha's meal preparations, which the Lord finds to be too extensive. Doing less in the kitchen would let her listen to his words and eliminate her jealousy of Mary. The passive sense of the word *perispao* supports this reading: that is, Martha *was pulled on*, or *dragged away* by her work. This reading, that Martha is doing too much busy work, is a common one, held by Reginald C. Fuller (1008), for example. What follows, then, is that the "one thing" necessary is literally one dish. A simple meal would be more appropriate for the Lord and his followers than the banquet Martha is presumably fussing about preparing.

Developing this line of interpretation somewhat differently, other commentators view the "one thing" as Jesus and his teachings—in other words, the necessary thing is the "better part" that Mary has chosen. Marshall reads the verse in this way and sees it as Martha's most important lesson (454). Adopting the same reading, Schweizer sees Jesus as carrying out the meal analogy and telling Martha implicitly that his word "provides a very different kind of nourishment" (189). Another dimension is suggested by Aelred Baker, who argues persuasively that this verse may be drawn from Psalm 27.4 and Sirach 11.10, which both use "one thing" articulations. Further, Baker cites Luke 18.22, the story of the rich young man, as another use of the "one thing" motif peculiar to Luke (136). It may also be possible that the "one thing" does not point forward to Mary's good choice but points back to Martha's being troubled about many things. Unlike Mary, who seemingly knows she belongs with the Lord, Martha is unfocused and unhappy. Though she has been the one to receive the Lord into her house, she seems to have gained little joy from it. Here we might contrast Martha with Zaccheus, who receives the Lord *joyfully* into his house and, as cause or effect, has gained salvation.

It should be noted that textual uncertainty on this point contributes to a variety of interpretations. Marshall notes that there are six variant forms of Jesus's answer to Martha, and all have adherents (452–53). The text may say "one thing is necessary" or "one thing, or few things are necessary" or "only a few things are necessary." However, most scholars seem to find the "one thing" reading most authentic and appropriate (Schweizer 189) because of its existence in the early documents and its other Lukan use.

The next section of the pronouncement evaluates Mary's action, that the part Mary has chosen is best. It is interesting to see that Mary is seen as active: she has *chosen* this part. The key word describing Martha, on the other hand, is passive: she *was pulled away* or *was distracted.* It is also important to notice that while Mary's part is best, there is no suggestion that Martha's part or role is necessarily bad. The text need not be seen as encouraging divisiveness between the sisters; indeed, it may be the opposite. Mary, the humble disciple, may be seen as embodying the lessons of love, while Martha, troubled and conflicted, has not gotten that "one thing" clarified for herself.

Mary's choice of role or activity, then, should not be taken from her, and will not be. With this, Luke's Jesus ends his pronouncement. It is easy to read this final statement as a rebuke to Martha. She has asked the Lord for a specific action, that he should send her sister in to help her. In that Martha wants to have something "fixed," in a sense, the pericope almost suggests a healing narrative. Is Martha healed, and if so, in what ways? She does not get the healing or change or repair that she has requested. But in fact, the last sentence may suggest that reconciliation or peace is to be the outcome. Mary's role is not to be taken from her, but that does not exclude Martha from sharing in that role. She asked Mary to join her in her role, but it may be that Martha is implicitly invited into Mary's "part" herself, just as the elder brother is invited into the feast for the Prodigal Son.

According to John Drury, Luke likes to show people experiencing "broken journeys" that result in "transforming crises" (427). It may be that Martha is experiencing such a crisis in this pericope. Such a reading seems more appropriate to the Gospel than one that is more negative toward the person who, at the least, enacts some hospitality. In any case, the fact that the text may support this and so many other contradictory interpretations is evidence of the richness of Luke's literary art and his profound insight into human nature.

Works Cited

Baker, Aelred. "One Thing Necessary." *Catholic Biblical Quarterly* 27 (1965): 127–37.

Bernhard, Sr., Thomas. "Women's Ministry in the Church: A Lukan Perspective." *St. Luke Journal of Theology* 29 (1986): 261–63.

Cassidy, Richard J. *Jesus, Politics, and Society: A Study of Luke's Gospel.* Maryknoll, NY: Orbis, 1978.

Corrington, Gail Patterson. *Her Image of Salvation: Female Saviors and Formative Christianity.* Louisville: Westminster/John Knox, 1992.

D'Angelo, Mary Rose. "Women in Luke-Acts: A Redactional View." *Journal of Biblical Literature* 109 (1990): 441–61.

Danker, Frederick W. *Luke.* Philadelphia: Fortress, 1976.

Douglas, J. D., ed. *The New Greek-English Interlinear New Testament.* Wheaton, IL: Tyndale, 1990.

Drury, John. "Luke." *The Literary Guide to the Bible.* Ed. Robert Alter and Frank Kermode. Cambridge, MA: Harvard UP, 1987. 418–39.

Edwards, O.C. *Luke's Story of Jesus.* Philadephia: Fortress, 1981.

Ellis, E. Earle. *The Gospel of Luke.* London: Nelson, 1966.

Erb, Peter C. "The Contemplative Life and the *Unum Necessarium:* In Defense of a Traditional Reading of Luke 10:42." *Mystics Quarterly* 11 (1985): 161–64.

Evans, Craig A. *New International Bible Commentary: Luke.* Peabody, MA: Hendrickson, 1990.

Fiorenza, Elisabeth Schüssler. "A Feminist Critical Interpretation for Liberation: Martha and Mary: Lk. 10:38–42." *Religion and Intellectual Life* 3 (1986): 21–36.

———. *In Memory of Her: A Feminist Theological Reconstruction of Christian Origins.* New York: Crossroad, 1988.

Fitzmyer, Joseph A. *The Gospel According to Luke.* Garden City, NY: Doubleday, 1983. Vol. 28 of The Anchor Bible.

Fuller, Reginald C., et al., eds. *A New Catholic Commentary on Holy Scripture.* London: Nelson, 1969.

Geldenhuys, Norval. *Commentary on the Gospel of Luke.* Grand Rapids, MI: Eerdmans, 1956.

Karris, Robert J. *Invitation to Luke.* Garden City, NY: Doubleday/Image, 1977.

Kopas, Jane. "Jesus and Women in Luke's Gospel." *Theology Today* 43 (1986): 192–202.

Lawton, David. *Faith, Text, and History: The Bible in English.* Charlottesville, VA: UP of Virginia, 1990.

"Luke." *The Interpreter's Bible.* 1952 ed.

Marshall, I. Howard. *The Gospel of Luke: A Commentary on the Greek Text.* Grand Rapids, MI: Eerdmans, 1978.

"Mary." *Anchor Bible Dictonary.* 1992 ed.

Meyer, Marvin W. "Making Mary Male: The Categories 'Male' and 'Female' in the Gospel of Thomas." *New Testament Studies* 31 (1985): 554–70.

Navone, John. "The Conversion Dynamic of Biblical Themes." *Studies in Formative Spirituality* 13 (1992): 323–31.

O'Rahilly, A. "The Two Sisters." *Scripture* 4 (1949): 68–76.

Parvey, Constance F. "Theology and Leadership of Women in the New Testament." *Religion and Sexism: Images of Woman in the Jewish and Christian Traditions.* Ed. Rosemary Radford Ruether. New York: Simon and Schuster, 1974. 117–49.

Powell, Mark Allan. *What Are They Saying about Luke?* New York: Paulist, 1989.

Prichard, John Paul. *A Literary Approach to the New Testament.* Norman: U of Oklahoma P, 1972.

Schaberg, Jane. "Luke." *The Women's Bible Commentary.* Ed. Carol A. Newsom and Sharon H. Ringe. Louisville: Westminster/John Knox, 1992. 275–92.

Schweizer, Eduard. *The Good News According to Luke.* Trans. David E. Green. Atlanta: John Knox, 1984.

Swartley, Willard M. "Politics or Peace (*Eirene*) in Luke's Gospel." *Political Issues in Luke-Acts.* Ed. Richard J. Cassidy and Philip J. Scharper. Maryknoll, NY.: Orbis, 1983. 18–37.

Sweetland, Dennis M. "The Good Samaritan and Mary and Martha." *Bible Today* 21 (1983): 325–30.

Talbert, Charles H. *Reading Luke: A Literary and Theological Commentary on the Third Gospel.* New York: Crossroad, 1982.

Thompson, G. H. P. *Commentary to the Gospel According to Luke in the RSV.* Oxford: Clarendon, 1972.

Via, E. Jane. "Women, the Discipleship of Service, and the Early Christian Ritual Meal." *St. Luke Journal of Theology* 29 (1985): 37–60.

Sample Paper in Chicago Style:
Phillis Wheatley: Singer in a Strange Land

The African child who would become the poet Phillis Wheatley appeared in the United States on a slave ship on July 11, 1761. Auctioned off in Boston with other captives a few weeks later, Phillis was purchased by Mrs. Susanna Wheatley.[1] Phillis was only about seven years old, but, as Richmond notes, Colonial ladies often were willing to buy very young slaves because, although they were not immediately useful, they were considered "unformed and malleable."[2] In any case, with Phillis, the Wheatley family had gotten a bargain. Within eighteen months, she had made herself a prodigy, reading and writing English and beginning to learn Latin.[3] She became a faithful friend, a humble housemaid—and the first published African American writer.[4] Widely viewed as a prodigy and a curiosity, Wheatley travelled with her mistress's daughter to England, met nobility, and published a widely reviewed, well-received book of verse.[5]

The world into which Phillis arrived was prosperous, pre-Revolutionary War Boston, a city whose roots lay deep in Puritanism. Justo L. González points out that new England Puritanism was evangelical, extending to the Indians.[6] Therefore, it ought not to be surprising that a kind of practical theology came about regarding slaves as Christians: the owner of slaves, especially first-generation slaves, could justify himself or herself by saying that the Africans' being enslaved was a small price to pay for the gift of being Christianized. M. A. Richmond believes that the pious Mrs. Susanna Wheatley, "confirmed in the Puritan belief in the immediacy and practicality of divine justice," would have believed that making Phillis into a good Christian and a good servant would have been nearly synonymous.[7] By the mid-nineteenth century, the abolition movement would center around Boston, but in Wheatley's day, the Christian convictions of most Bostonians did not extend to any equality of treatment for African Americans.[8] As William H. Robinson notes, blacks could attend church (sitting in the rear) and be baptized, but baptism in no way altered the fact of their slavery.[9]

In 1771, Wheatley became a member of the Old South Congregational Church, to which her "family," the Wheatleys, all belonged; several pastors of that congregation would later befriend Wheatley and become the subjects of her poetry.[10] But another religious influence on her poetry was the Great Awakening. As González summarizes it, this movement had emerged in Massachusetts in 1734 as a "Pietistic wave" that caused people to experience an emotional conversion.[11] Jonathan Edwards, an early leader of the movement, had "de-cisively departed from old Puritanism by his appropriation of the new psychology of sensation."[12] Wheatley's verse shows influence of the older Congregationalist Puritanism as well as the more fervent piety of George Whitefield and the Great Awakening.

But more importantly, Wheatley's verse shows the tension between her life as an artist creating typical Neoclassical verse, and her life as a slave—however privileged and comfortable, a slave nonetheless. One usually thinks of slavery as synonymous with the Southern plantation system, the brutal overseer, and the illiterate slave. Wheatley suffered none of these evils; she lived comfortably with her "family."[13] But the fact of her enslavement was still present, however silken the bonds holding her. The brilliant "child" of an intensely religious household, Wheatley had the intellectual and contextual tools to confront the dichotomy of her life and the duplicity of the Puritans' practice of slavery. This confrontation occurs, subtly, in many of her religious poems, in their themes and image patterns.

Wheatley's most famous poem is "On Being Brought from Africa to America":

> 'Twas mercy brought me from my Pagan land,
> Taught my benighted soul to understand
> That there's a God, that there's a Saviour too:
> Once I redemption neither sought nor knew,
> Some view our sable race with scornful eye;
> "Their colour is a diabolic dye."
> Remember, Christians, Negroes, black as Cain,
> May be refin'd, and join th' angelic train.[14]

This poem, read on a surface level, seems to acquiesce in the slaveholders' justification of slavery as evangelical opportunity, and indeed such a reading of the poem is responsible for African American and women's studies scholars' coming to an appreciation of Wheatley only rather recently. S. E. Ogude articulates this earlier assessment of Wheatley, referring to her "dry rationalization of the Christian faith" and her "repugnant" thought.[15] But critics today argue that Wheatley, as Silvers puts it, "learned to write *like* a European" but not *"as* a European."[16] As James A. Levernier claims, Wheatley is in fact creating a "far different message" from the surface sense.[17] The poem is laden with "irony" and "an intentionally misleading symbolic pattern" that allows her a protest otherwise closed to her in a racist society.[18]

Sondra O'Neale's richly revisionist reading of this poem goes further into these issues; she points out that, while the colonialist would expect a usual Puritan dichotomy of black versus white equalling good versus evil, Wheatley "moves her images of the darkness and the 'diabolic dye' from dark skin…to a heightened and totally spiritual and evangelical worldview whereby anyone who has not heard and received the gospel…is in darkness." Furthermore, O'Neale notes that Wheatley's use of "Saviour" in addition to "God" functions for a biblically literate audience as a reminder that "Saviour" is the word used for the God who brings the Israelites out of slavery.[19] William J. Scheick points out another subversive Biblical allusion, in the word "refin'd," which he hears as echoing Isaiah 48:10 in the King James Version: "Behold, I have refined thee, but not with silver; I have chosen thee in the furnace of affliction."[20] Thus, Wheatley associates herself and other blacks with a virtue that comes not just from conversion to Christianity, but with the "refinement" of the suffering people of God. This move is quite a dramatic one—one that requires the reader to switch from seeing the black slaves as bearing a curse inherited from Cain, to seeing the slaves as chosen people, suffering now, but, in the necessary corollary, inevitably redeemed by the Saviour.

These comments have dealt with how the poem achieves its subversive purpose; a further issue to raise is the nature of the theology proposed by this poem, and by Wheatley overall. An overview of her work, with special attention to the poem cited above, reveals a theology based upon the liberating power of God the "Saviour." At the same time, a tension emerges as Wheatley struggles with the Puritan version of what it is to be human. She resolves these conflicts through creating a public voice that echoes those of other Neoclassical writers such as Alexander Pope and Samuel Johnson, satirists who reproach the reader for falling short of the ideal of reason that the era espouses.

Other poems reveal Wheatley's concept of authority through the voice she creates. Phillip Richards singles out these lines:

'Twas not long since I left my native shore
The land of errors, and Egyptian gloom:
Father of mercy, 'twas thy gracious hand
Brought me in safety from those dark abodes.[21]

These lines are clearly the sort of thing that has caused readers to see Wheatley as wholly accommodationist to her own slavery, but Richards argues that in fact Wheatley is claiming authority here: She can chastise those who would be seen as her "social betters" because she has "firsthand experience of the deadly nature of sin." He goes on to argue that Wheatley is claiming, "in the best possible Puritan manner, an experiential knowledge of the central spiritual and moral realities."[22] Of course, the irony of the passage is in the fact that Wheatley treats Africa as the "Egypt" in which she was a slave to sin; thus, her freedom (from sin) came when she was enslaved.

Yet Wheatley's other writings clearly show that she cherished a passion for liberty, for herself and others. Levernier has argued that Wheatley learned an antislavery stance not only from her own experience as a slave but from her New England pastors, who were all patriots, advocates of the American Revolution. From them, she heard "impassioned pleas concerning the innate rights of all humans to personal liberty,"[23] which must have spoken to her in ways the speakers perhaps did not intend.

For Wheatley, Puritanism was simultaneously attractive and disastrous. Richmond argues effectively that the essence of Puritanism was inappropriate for a slave:

[The slave is] outside of those premises and compensations to which Puritanism appealed for its validity. Property and its acquisition, the...rewards of thrift and abstinence, were not for slaves...The full measure of self-reliance was a paradox to the essential dependency of slaves. What blacks were offered was the theology, disembodied from its temporal matrix."[24]

An excerpt from a letter to the Rev. Samson Occom reveals Wheatley's struggle to reconcile her experience and her received theology:

> Divine Light is chasing away the thick Darkness which broods over the Land of Africa; and the Chaos which has reign'd so long, is converting into beautiful Order, and reveals more and more clearly, the glorious Dispensation of civil and religious liberty, which are so inseparably united, that there is little or no enjoyment of one without the other...in every human Breast, God has implanted a Principle, which we call love of Freedom; it is impatient of Oppression, and pants for deliverance.[25]

Much of the language here is reminiscent of Puritanism; Wheatley is trying to use the tools of the established order to make it see the need to reform itself. Wheatley goes on in the letter to point out a failure of reason on the part of those who cry for liberty for the Colonies but still oppress others. Surely the appeal to reason, to a Neoclassical audience, would bear fruit.

But it did not, of course, at least not in Wheatley's lifetime. Freed at the Wheatleys' deaths, she discovered that the immense early audience for her poetry, for the novelty of a "colored" Latin scholar and poet, had diminished. She married an impoverished man, had a number of children who died young, and was dead herself at thirty-one.

The tragedy of Wheatley's life cannot be allowed to eclipse her achievements as a poet and as a religious thinker. While she may not be a thoroughgoing systematic theologian, her accomplishments in that area are still impressive, especially considering the confines in which she had to speak. Looking at all her poems and letters, one finds an intertext of sadness and inner conflict from a writer who would always be an outsider in her own culture—and who, until recently, was scorned by contemporary scholars as having been accommodationist, apolitical, and insensitive to the plight of other African Americans. But today we are learning to read Wheatley right, to discern the complexity of her vision and the sometimes encoded nature through which she had to convey that vision.

Endnotes

[1]William H. Robinson, *Phillis Wheatley and Her Writings* (New York: Garland, 1984), 5.

[2]M. A. Richmond, *Bid the Vassal Soar: Interpretative Essays on the Life and Poetry of Phillis Wheatley and George Moses Horton* (Washington, DC: Howard University Press, 1974), 14.

[3]Robinson, 22.

[4]Joanna Russ, in *How to Suppress Women's Writing* (Austin: University of Texas Press, 1983), has argued that labeling a female artist as "first" and afterward ignoring her is one way unsympathetic critics have detracted attention from her accomplishments (68). Russ sees Wheatley and her near-contemporary Anne Bradstreet as victims of this practice.

[5]Robinson, 33–36. For an account of the reception of her book, see Mukhtar Ali Isani, "The British Reception of Wheatley's *Poems on Various Subjects*," *Journal of Negro History* 66 (1982): 144–49. Isani points out that all the reviews were positive, but most reviewers were more impressed by Wheatley's achievement in view of her race and enslavement than they were by the achievement itself (144).

[6]Justo L. González, *The Story of Christianity: Vol. 2, The Reformation to the Present Day* (San Francisco: HarperSanFrancisco, 1985), 224.

[7]Richmond, 19.

[8]There was, however, a nascent movement in Wheatley's day; see Roger Bruns, ed., *Am I Not a Man and a Brother: The Antislavery Crusade of Revolutionary America* (New York: Chelsea House, 1977). The extent to which Wheatley was in touch with this movement is, like much of her life, unknown.

[9]Robinson, 11. Robinson goes on to note that the baptism of blacks was held only after other services were concluded (18). See also Lorenzo Johnston Greene, *The Negro in Colonial New England* (Port Washington, NY: Kennikat Press, 1942), 257–89.

[10]Ibid., 18–19. But for a discussion of Wheatley as a Methodist, see Samuel J. Rogal, "Phillis Wheatley's Methodist Connection," *Black American Literature Forum* 21 (1987): 85–95.

[11]González, 228.

[12]Perry Miller, *Errand into the Wilderness* (Cambridge, Mass.: Belknap/Harvard University Press, 1956), 182.

[13]Richmond (19–20) points out that Phillis was "coddled," allowed the rare privilege of keeping a fire burning at all times in her room so that she could write in comfort at any hour. Richmond also notes, however, the psychological price Wheatley probably paid: in a household with many slaves, she was inevitably alienated from them and, of course, would never have been completely accepted as an equal by those who, however civilly, still owned her.

[14]Phillis Wheatley, *Poems on Various Subjects, Religious and Moral* (Philadelphia: Joseph Crukshank, 1786. Reprint, New York: AMS Press, 1976), 13.

[15]S. E. Ogude, "Slavery and the African Imagination," *World Literature Today* 55 (1981): 21.

[16]Anita Silvers, "Pure Historicism and the Heritage of Hero(in)es: Who Grows in Phillis Wheatley's Garden?" *Journal of Aesthetics and Art Criticism* 51 (1993): 476.

[17]James A. Levernier, "Wheatley's 'On Being Brought from Africa to America,'" *Explicator* 40 (1981): 25.

[18]James A. Levernier, "Style as Protest in the Poetry of Phillis Wheatley," *Style* 27 (1993): 181.

[19]Sondra O'Neale, "A Slave's Subtle War: Phillis Wheatley's Use of Biblical Myth and Symbol," *Early American Literature* 21 (1987): 148.

[20]William J. Scheick, "Phillis Wheatley's Appropriation of Isaiah," *Early American Literature* 27 (1992): 136.

[21]Quoted in Phillip Richards, "Phillis Wheatley and Literary Americanization," *American Quarterly* 44 (1992): 178.

[22]Ibid., 179.

[23]James A. Levernier, "Phillis Wheatley and the New England Clergy," *Early American Literature* 26 (1991): 23.

[24]Richmond, 65.

[25]Quoted in Bruns, 307–8.

CHAPTER 5

A Brief Manual of Usage

Grammar, Usage, and Mechanics

Many people who struggle as writers or as speakers are wrestling not so much with ideas and development as they are with the aspect that English teachers sometimes call GUM: grammar, usage, and mechanics. But before we begin examining these issues, let's think about their implications. Some of us grew up in a setting in which standard English grammar was not used, and we all managed to communicate quite well regardless. Others of us took in standard English from our earliest acquisition of language. None of this, of course, matters in the least to God. Our linguistic "correctness" has nothing to do with our faith lives or our overall ability to minister. However, we may find that in some settings, our communication with others will be hindered unless we have the option of using standard written and spoken English. This section is intended to aid you in improving your ability to command standard discourse in speech and writing. Learning what's in this chapter will not make you a better person, but it may help you to be more confident of your ability to communicate. So let's take a quick look at some common trouble spots and try to get rid of some sticky GUM problems![1]

We'll begin with a very common problem in writing, difficulties with sentence recognition. If your teachers ever marked "frag" or "cs" or "run-on" in the margins of your paper, you were having problems in this area.

Recognizing Whole Sentences

Sentence fragments, comma splices, and run-on sentences are all errors of sentence recognition. If you make any of these errors, you may feel somewhat dismayed to think that you are not, at this point in your life, even able to recognize a sentence. But don't despair. You probably are doing fine at recognizing almost all sentences, but one or two particular kinds trip you up. Let's look at some common errors and the particular kinds of sentence structures that cause many writers to fall into error.

A *sentence fragment* is a cluster of words that does not form a full grammatical sentence but is punctuated as though it did. A *comma splice* or a *run-on sentence* (also called a fused or run- together sentence) is the opposite of a fragment. When you write a fragment, you are punctuating an incomplete sentence as though it were complete; when you write a comma splice or a fused sentence, you are punctuating two or more sentences as though they were only one sentence. Let's take a closer look at these problems and try to find helpful ways to get rid of them.

The basic unit of real communication is not the individual word but the sentence (whole thought). "Life" says something to us, but "Christ gives life" says more. Those three words comprise a whole sentence: subject, verb, object. A sentence is a grammatical unit and a thought unit. However, of those two terms, we give precedence to the sentence as grammatical unit. If I write "He gives life," I've written a full grammatical sentence, even though as a thought unit, the sentence falls short (the pronoun subject lacks specificity). We need to be aware of the grammatical unit, because that unit will determine what punctuation is needed.

---

[1]This section is intended as an overview of common problems. Should you need more intensive help, see some of the resources listed at the end of this chapter.

The first rule we'll look at is the one that says sentences always should be punctuated and/or capitalized in such a way that we're showing we know they are sentences. Usually a sentence starts with a capital letter and ends with a period; however, there are exceptions. A whole thought can end with other end marks, such as question marks and exclamation points. Also, whole thoughts can be linked together within the same boundaries of capital to period. They may be linked through a variety of methods, including semicolons, colons, and conjunctions. Take a look at these examples:

> My first-year seminary classes were challenging; they really kept me busy.

> My first-year seminary classes were challenging, so they really kept me busy.

> My first-year seminary classes were challenging: they really kept me busy.

Any of these options would be fine, because either a semicolon or colon creates the appropriate boundary between the two individual thought units, as does the conjunction *so,* preceded by the comma. What is *not* acceptable is using the comma without the conjunction. This misuse of the comma as an end mark constitutes the error called a "comma splice" or "comma fault," one of the more egregious errors in sentence recognition. At some point in your writing career, many of you have had a red circle marked on a paper, with the mysterious note "cs" written above it. What was a "cs," and how were you to fix it? Now you know. A comma splice is simply the error of "splicing" or connecting two sentences with a comma, a punctuation mark too weak to do the job. Where you had a comma, you should have had one of the options shown above.

In order to avoid comma splices, or find them and correct them in your revision process, you need to have three skills. First, you need to *recognize a complete sentence.* The good news here is that almost everyone has this skill. Second, you need to *know alternatives* to the comma-splice construction. As you have just seen, there are many alternatives to the comma splice: You can substitute a semicolon, add a conjunction (joining word), or even break the thought into two sentences. Third, you need to have a reliable method of re-seeing (*revising*) your writings (see chapter 2) so that you'll catch the error if it occurs. Let's take a closer look at ways we can find and revise these errors.

Most of us are pretty uncreative in our errors. Our habits of thought and expression lead us to the same sentence constructions, whether they are good or not so good, again and again. Comma splices tend to occur in certain kinds of sentences, so let's look at those kinds of sentences. Then you can assess your own habits and discover under what circumstances you commonly make these errors. Comma splices usually occur in two types of sentence pairs: those in which the second whole thought begins with a pronoun, and those in which the second whole thought begins with a false joining word. It's easy to see how we can fall into these errors; in both cases, the two separate grammatical units logically seem to be one. Therefore, we need to look closely at these structures and become able to create them correctly as we write and revise.

Take a look at these sentences:

Rev. Davis is looking for a new pastorate. He is hoping to be in a larger church.

A faith life needs community; it can't prosper in a vacuum.

My church history paper is finished, and now I can work on my homiletics assignment.

These three sentences offer examples of structures in which the second full thought begins with a pronoun. In such sentences, writers often mistakenly use commas to join the thoughts. Look at the sentences, listen to their rhythms, and become aware that where a semicolon or a period is used, a comma would not be correct. In other words, recognize that in each sample, there are two sentences that should either be joined with a semicolon, separated into two sentences with a period, or more fully joined by the addition of a conjunction.

Comma splices also occur in structures such as these:

Stewardship is a hard subject for a sermon; nonetheless, sometimes we must preach on it.

Many scholars believe the gospel of Mark was written in Rome; however, others disagree.

I believe I was called by God to the ministry. Therefore, I must follow that call.

Notice that the second thought unit in these three sentences begins with a transitional word (*nonetheless, therefore,* and *however*) that functions to link the two thoughts and show relationship between them. But notice, too, that the link is incomplete; therefore, the two thought units remain grammatically separate and should be acknowledged as such by separation into two sentences (see the third example) or by use of a semicolon. Because the link is incomplete, those transitional words are often called "false joining words." In addition to the three cited above, false joining words and phrases include *then, on the other hand, nevertheless, also,* and *in addition.* False joining words are not to be confused with true joining words, seven conjunctions that can in fact join two thoughts with the aid of just a comma. The seven true conjunctions are these: *and, but, or, nor, for, so,* and *yet.*

We often become confused because, as you probably have seen, the false joining words seem to have the same meaning as some of the true ones. It is correct to write, "I saved my money, but I still had trouble buying my texts." Omitting the word *but* and inserting *however,* I now have to write, "I saved my money; however, I still had trouble buying my texts." When the two sound almost alike, why should they demand different punctuation? Simple. Even though *however* neatly takes the place of *but* in the sentence above, it is merely impersonating a joining word. You can find out if a word is truly a joining word by seeing if it can be moved. A true joining word can't be anyplace other than between the two thoughts to be joined. Try reading the sentence above with *but* in any other position. "I saved my money; I still but had trouble buying my texts"? Nope. Now try it with *however:* "I saved my money; I still, however, had trouble buying my texts." It makes sense. *However* can be in several different spots in the second thought because it is commenting on the second thought, not really connecting the two. The same is true of all the false joining words. Try moving them around.

Now that I've convinced you of the trickiness of these words, I hope your awareness will make you more alert to the need to revise and catch these problems. Search for these words and then look carefully at the sentences in which they occur. If you find problems, use one of the options above to correct the error.

Sentence Fragments

A fragment is a cluster of words punctuated as though it were a whole sentence. Occasionally, a writer will write a fragment intentionally, for emphasis, but most formal writing calls for consistent use of whole sentences. If your writing has sometimes used unintentional incomplete sentences, you need to improve by applying the three steps outlined above: Recognize the problem, know ways to fix it, and use a revising process that will let you fix it.

In order to recognize the problem, you need to be looking for the particular problems you have. There are varied kinds of sentence recognition problems, and most people have only one or two kinds. Most people who create fragments write added-thought fragments. These fragments happen when the writer follows up one idea with another significant supporting idea and lets the supporting idea stand alone as a sentence, even though it is not. The significance of the idea deters the writer from seeing that it is not grammatically whole. For example, you might write, "It is easy for the pastor to neglect personal prayer. The reason being that she is overwhelmed by demands on her time." I hope you recognize that, in spite of its good and interesting idea, the second unit is not a whole sentence. If you listen to it, you hear its close relationship to the preceding sentence; in grammatical terms, it lacks a main verb. Replacing the *-ing* verb *being* with *is* solves the problem, and now you can probably hear that the sentence is complete. However, revising to get rid of fragments should open the door to all sorts of revising for better sentences, so you might realize that "the reason is" is a waste of words, and a better construction might be something like, "Because she is overwhelmed by demands on her time, a pastor may neglect personal prayer," or "A pastor may neglect personal prayer if she is overwhelmed by demands on her time." Many other revisions are possible. What you need to do is to find a revision that solves the fragment problem and fits into the style of the writing. Of course, your doing that depends on your commitment to looking for those fragments in your writing! We all get into habits, good and bad, in our self-expression. Our individual minds tend to create certain formulations. So if one "the reason being" fragment is pointed out to you, you need to red-flag that phrase and looking for it on your own. Doing a word search is a good idea, just to be on the safe side. This is one way a computer can be an outstanding aid. Using a grammar check in your word processing program also helps, but such checks are extremely uneven in quality, and they miss many errors. If you have sentence recognition problems or problems with awkward sentences, you will likely find it helpful to read your writing aloud, *sentence by sentence.* If you read slowly and carefully, your ear will help you find problems your eye might miss.

Now that we have examined some basics about full sentences, let's turn our attention to common grammatical problems within sentences. These have to do with our choices of pronouns and verbs.

Problem Pronouns

Pronouns, as you probably learned in school, are words that stand in place of a noun (a person, place, or thing). Pronouns create problems for us because they change depending on their role in a sentence. Thus, pronouns can be labeled according to *how many* people or things they stand for (*number,* singular or plural) and *what role* they play in the sentence (*case*). There are other labels, too, but we won't worry about them right now.

Most of us know how to avoid the most egregious errors of pronoun use. For example, we probably all know that it's incorrect to say, "Deacon Jackson and me went to the district meeting." In grammatical terms, *me* is in the objective case; that is, it's used as an object in a sentence. In the sample sentence, the pronoun called for, *I,* would be the one appropriate for the subject of a sentence, not the object.

Many glaring grammatical errors occur when someone uses the objective in place of the nominative (subject) case, as the example above shows. But a resulting problem is *overcorrection*. This difficulty occurs when we are so worried about using the objective case wrongly that we instead don't use it when we should. Therefore, we might say something like "The deacon passed the collection plate to Clare and I." Looking at this from a grammatical stance, we recognize that "Clare and I" functions as the (compound) object of the preposition *to;* therefore, *I* can't be correct, because it is used as a subject, not an object. *Me* is the objective form, so the sentence should read, "He passed the collection plate to Clare and me." And while we all know that "Us deacons went to a workshop last Saturday" is not correct, we are somewhat more in doubt about "The advice given to us deacons was helpful." "*Us* deacons"? "*We* deacons"? You might be tempted simply to recast the sentence as "We all got good advice," which is a perfectly good option! But it's best to know the correct choices and revise for clearer meaning, not out of uncertainty about grammatical choices. In this case, the rules are easy. In the phrase "The advice given to us deacons," *us* is the right choice because *us* is in the objective case and is the object of the preposition *to.* What throws us off in such a sentence is the presence of *deacons,* which here functions as an appositive (a noun or pronoun that identifies the preceding noun or pronoun, such as "my friend Jeff" or "our pastor, Rev. Baker"). But all we have to remember about this situation is that the appositive structure doesn't change the grammatical need: If the sentence should read "The advice given to us," it should also read "The advice given to us deacons."

You'll notice that pronoun problems often occur when a sentence uses plurals. None of us would ever say or write, "He passed the plate to I" or "Me went to the district conference." If you remember that case doesn't change just because another word has been added, you will probably be less likely to make errors in this area.

A very tricky area of pronoun choice occurs when we use "than" plus a pronoun. Of the following two sentences, which do you think is correct: "Marianne likes Jeff more than me" or "Marianne likes Jeff more than I"? I warned you that this would be tricky! The answer is that both are potentially correct. Which you choose depends on your meaning. The *than* is introducing a clause in which words are left out. The sentence above may mean "Marianne likes Jeff more than (she likes) me" or "Marianne likes Jeff more than I (like Jeff)." Most sentences, however, are less ambiguous than the example above. If you're in doubt, just think what words are being omitted: for example, "Rev. Masters is taller than I (am)." Once you know these rules and structures, just a little thought will usually solve the pronoun problems.

Speakers and writers are often confused by *who* and *whom*. In grammatical terms, *who* is used as a subject and *whom* as an object. The *-m* ending of *whom* should remind you that *whom*, like *him* and *them*, serves as an object (*whoever* and *whomever* are used in the same ways). If you don't remember a lot of grammar, this explanation probably does not help much, so let's try another method: Think of *who/whom* as being part of a question, and *he/him* as being the answer. If the answer is *he*, you want *who* in the question; if the answer is *him*, you want *whom*. Here are some examples:

> "Whoever, therefore, eats the bread or drinks the cup...[*He* eats the bread.] (1 Cor. 11:27)

> "The pastor whom we hire must be a person of mature faith." [We hire *him*.]

> "The strangers (who the readers know are God and angels) come to dinner to deliver a message: God promises Abraham and Sarah that the barren will rejoice."[2] [The reader knows *they* are God and angels.]

Another troubling aspect of pronoun use is the possessive. With nouns, the possessive case is fairly simple: We usually just add the apostrophe and *s*. But with pronouns, the opportunity for error is unfortunately greater. (The good news is that these errors are not apparent in speech!) Let's look at a few issues in possessive pronoun use.

---

[2]Mary W. Anderson, "Hospitality Theology," *Christian Century* 115 (1998): 635.

First, note that we need to use a possessive pronoun before a gerund. If you don't know grammar, the preceding sentence probably doesn't help you a lot, so let's define the terms. Possessive pronouns include *my, your, his, her, its, their,* and *our.* They stand before nouns to show possession or relationship. Gerunds are verbs with *-ing* endings that are playing the role of nouns (things) in a sentence. For example, "Golfing detracts from church attendance." In that sentence, *golfing* is treated as a thing; it's the subject of the sentence. Therefore, it could have a possessive pronoun before it, as in "Our golfing" or "Our playing golf kept us from attending church." Listen to these sentences and catch the pattern of correct use:

"His bullying the other members of the board was outrageous."

"We were all delighted with their offering to help with the bazaar."

"My finding a role in ministry involved a long struggle."

A last and important word about possessive pronouns: *They do not take apostrophes.* Some people want to stick an apostrophe in a pronoun just because it has an *s* at the end. Don't do that! Here are some correct examples:

"This hymnal is his. That hymnal is yours, and those hymnals are theirs."

Notice that there are no apostrophes. The word *its* is probably the most problematical in this area. *Its* is a genderless possessive pronoun. If we don't know the sex of a kitten, we call it "it." And we would say, "The kitten hurt its paw." Note that there is no apostrophe in "its." One way to remember this is to think of "its" as analogous to "his." If we find out that the kitten is male, we say, "his paw." There's no apostrophe in "his," nor is there one in "its." Putting an incorrect apostrophe in "its" is one of the most common punctuation errors.

Why is this error so common? The reason is simple: Sometimes we do put an apostrophe in "its," and it's correct. In fact, the preceding sentence is an example. *It's,* correctly used, is not a possessive pronoun but the contraction of "it is" or "it has." Look at the following sentences; all are correct:

"It's been a long day."

"My new car is saving me money; its gas mileage is terrific."

"The effectiveness of a paragraph can often be measured by its unity."

"It's going to take time for me to improve my prayer life."

"Euphoria hit early on, as it often does in religious conversion, but I found that its passing did not weaken my newfound faith."[3]

If you are ever unsure whether *it's* or *its* is correct, there is an easy test to apply. Just reread the sentence with "it is" or "it has" in place of "it's." If it sounds stupid ("I listened to his sermon, but I must have missed *it is* point"), you know you want the possessive pronoun *its* with no apostrophe. If you know you have made errors with the "it's/its" distinction in the past, just remember the test, and commit yourself to checking for this problem as part of your revising process.

Another common error is omitting the possessive before a gerund. Let's look at some examples of how the possessive in this context is done correctly:

Greg's missing his church history final will ruin his grade.

Althea's questioning of Anselm's theology led to a good discussion.

Father Davis' visiting with the Baker family helped them a lot.

The disciples' misunderstanding of Jesus is evident in the gospels.

---

[3]Kathleen Norris, *Amazing Grace* (New York: Riverhead Books, 1998), 104.

Verb Problems

Older folks, and some younger ones, will recall having been taught the "principal parts" of verbs. Reciting "write, wrote, written" and "bring, brought, brought" may ring a bell for some of you. Most verb problems have to do with errors in choosing the right "principal part" or in failing to choose verbs that agree with subjects. Let's look at each of these areas.

With regard to principal parts, we have to admit that our wonderful, rich, expressive English language sometimes just doesn't make sense! Why should one set of principal parts be "ring, rang, rung" or "sing, sang, sung," and the next be "bring, brought, brought"? The problems arise from our language's varied origins, which have left us with many verbs categorized as "regular"–that is, ending with *ed* to form the principal parts ("walk, walked, walked")–while others are "irregular," forming their principal parts by internal changes. As little children acquiring language, we tend to make all verbs regular ("I goed" instead of "I went"). As adults, we sometimes still trip over some of the tricky verbs. All we can do is learn the standard choices and then revise to be sure we've used them correctly. Let's begin with a review of what the principal parts are all about.

When we hear a verb in its infinitive form ("to choose") we are also hearing its present tense ("today I *choose*"), which is the first of the three principal parts. The second of the three is the simple past tense ("yesterday I *chose*"), and finally the third ("in the past I have *chosen*") is the past participle. Confusion between the second and third causes most of our problems with verb form. Many people say or write "I have chose," mistaking the past tense for the past participle. Awareness and practice can help with this problem. Remember that the past participle form occurs only when the verb is accompanied by another verb, called an auxiliary or "helping" verb. Here's a brief list of commonly mistaken verbs and their principal parts:[4]

---

[4]If you are in doubt about what form is correct, check a dictionary, which will generally give the principal parts for any verb. This use is yet another reason to equip yourself with a good-quality desk dictionary!

Present	Past	Past Participle
see	saw	seen
write	wrote	written
give	gave	given
do	did	done
ride	rode	ridden
bring	brought	brought
go	went	gone

If you are like most people, just a few of these trip you up. Some people are in the habit of saying (or writing) "I seen" or "I have saw." Again, awareness and revision are the key to change. Practice saying "I saw" and "I have seen" and practice writing these forms correctly, and soon they will become habits.

The second problem area for verbs has to do with *agreement* in number between subject and verb. Most of us know that to say "The elder and the deacon is quarrelling" or "The two deacons is quarrelling" would be incorrect. In grammatical terms, we note that the subject is compound ("the elder and the deacon") or plural ("the two deacons") and therefore we need the plural verb "are." If you make errors in these sentence structures, be aware of this tendency, and revise to correct it.

More tricky are sentences in which the structure is less clear. These include sentences in which the subject follows the verb and those in which the subject and verb are separated by lengthy interrupting phrases. Another problem is sentences that use subjects joined with *or,* in which case the verb agrees with the closest object. Even though we may ordinarily have few problems with agreement, such sentences can be confusing. Let's look at a few examples:

The minister, along with the board chair and two elders, *is* attending the conference. ("Minister" is the sole subject.)

When building projects or even a minor repair *is* on the agenda, board meetings are lively. ("Repair" is the subject closest to the verb in this *or* structure.)

A desire to do God's will and love our neighbors is a key ingredient to ministry. ("Desire" is the subject.)

Common Punctuation Problems

Imagine trying to read a book with no periods, no commas, no capital letters, no paragraph indentations, none of the markers that we unconsciously rely on to guide us in our reading. The words would all be there, but nothing else. Such an experience of reading would quickly teach us that the aspects of "mechanical correctness" named above do indeed matter, and conforming to those standards is part of our obligation to our readers.

COMMAS

Commas are probably the most annoying punctuation mark, because they are used in many different settings and are often optional. Although it is difficult to come up with rigid rules for comma use, we can and should learn some guidelines.

- Commas separate complete clauses *if* the clauses are connected with a coordinating conjunction or true joining word (see pp. 86–90 on comma splices). There are only seven coordinating conjunctions (*and, but, or, nor, so, for, yet*), so it is not hard to recognize them. The preceding sentence provides an example of correct use of a comma with a conjunction.

- Commas set off opening thoughts from the rest of the sentence. Opening thoughts may be prepositional phrases ("In my time, I've seen a lot of changes in this seminary"), participle phrases ("Returning from class, I realized I'd forgotten to turn in my exegesis paper"), or dependent clauses ("When we meet God intimately in our everyday lives, we are forever changed").

- Commas set off interrupting or transitional words or phrases ("Martin Luther, on the other hand, had a different sense of the Eucharist" and "Let's turn our attention, then, to the Letter of Paul to the Romans").

- Commas set off items in a series ("Requirements for Dr. Dowd's class included research papers, readings, reports, and two exams").

- Commas set off nonessential clauses or phrases ("My pastor, who also attended this seminary, recently retired"). But note that phrases or clauses essential to the meaning are *not* set off. Look at this sentence: "All the seminary students who were enrolled in Dr. Smith's class were well prepared for their comprehensive exams." Were *all* of the seminary's students enrolled in Dr. Smith's class and therefore well prepared? Not according to the punctuation of this sentence. The "who were" clause is essential, restricting the meaning of "all the seminary students."

- Commas are conventionally used in separating the day and year in dates (January 3, 1958); in separating titles from names (Rev. Andrew Harnack, Jr.,); and in separating names of cities and states (Shreveport, Louisiana).

Comma use can be confusing for us, because some of the rules above are somewhat flexible. For example, while we normally do place a comma between two whole clauses joined by a conjunction, we may omit the comma if the clauses are short: "I've sinned and I've been forgiven." The same concept applies to short opening thoughts. You may write, "In my lifetime I've seen a lot of changes" either with or without the comma after "lifetime." I decide whether I will use the comma by deciding how I would read the sentence aloud. The comma creates the written equivalent of a vocal pause, so if I want to slow the reader down and draw emphasis with that pause, I'll use the comma.

Apostrophes

There are some fairly simple rules to learn about this useful little mark of punctuation. Essentially, it is used for two purposes: to show possession and to show contraction. You probably knew that already, so let's move on to the occasions when writers are likely to use this mark incorrectly. When using an apostrophe in a contraction, be aware that *the apostrophe goes in the spot where the contraction happens.* We contract "did not" as "didn't," and the apostrophe is placed where we contracted "not" into "n't."

Second, we use apostrophes to show possession: "Rev. Plummer's desk," "the church's carpeting," "the women's Bible study," or "the storm's wrath." The use of the apostrophe to show possession is fairly simple most of the time, but it can get a bit complicated when we are using plural possessives or need to show possession with words ending in *s*. Let's look briefly at these potential trouble spots.

If I am writing about one student and her study carrel, I write "Beth's study carrel" or "the student's study carrel." If several students are sharing the carrel, I write "their carrel" or "the students' carrel." Notice that in the first instance, the *s* on *student* was there merely to show the possessive. In the second case, the *s* was to show that there was more than just one student. The *s*, then, was part of the word. When I added the apostrophe to make it possessive, I added it at the end of the whole word. Remembering that the basic word is *students* and that the apostrophe is added to show possession will help you know where to place the mark.

The same idea will help you punctuate names ending in *s* or similar sounds. If you are referring to one church, you write "the church's foundations," but if you are referring to more than one, it's "the churches' foundations." If you remember that *churches* is the plural form and that the apostrophe is just added to make the plural possessive, you'll punctuate it correctly. The same principle applies to odd plural forms like *men's* and *children's*. For names ending in *s*, you have options. Most writers prefer "Charles's house" to "Charles' house," but either is correct. Traditionally, we add only the apostrophe to the names of Jesus and Moses. We use phrases like "in Jesus' name we pray" and "Moses' power to lead the Israelites."

A further use of the apostrophe is to add clarity when we use letters or numbers as word units. For example, we might write "Mind your p's and q's" or "I don't think 13's are unlucky."

But do be aware that we do *not* use the apostrophe at random for any unusual plural. If you choose to place your family's name over your front door or on your mailbox, use the simple plural "the Wilcoxes" or "the Smiths." No apostrophe is needed.

OTHER MARKS

If you have command of commas and apostrophes, plus the basic end marks of punctuation (periods and occasional question marks and exclamation points), you can get along pretty well in most writing. But let's take a quick look at a few other marks that will be handy. First, *quotation marks:* These are used to set off direct quotations or words used in a special sense. These marks can be tricky on occasion, mostly with regard to other marks. If you have been paying attention to my examples, you've perhaps noticed that periods and commas remain inside quotations, while colons and semicolons go outside. There's no real reason behind this. It's just a custom that most American writing observes.

Next, let's look at *dashes.* Formed by two hyphens, the dash sets off an interrupting or dramatic thought. Be aware that the dash is often overused. Proofread your formal writings and be sure that the mark is appropriate.

Colons are also frequently misused. Appropriately, they begin lists, but only *after* a complete thought. "For church camp you need to bring the following items: a flashlight, insect repellent, a bathing suit, toiletries, and five changes of clothing." Notice that a whole sentence ends with the word "items." The misuse of the colon happens when writers suspend the sentence at "bring" and place the colon there.

A Glossary of Problem Words

Affect/effect: Almost always, *affect* is a verb and *effect* is a noun. Look at these sentences: "How will these changes affect our church? Well, the effect is likely to be minimal."

A lot: People commonly spell this as one word, but in your writing you should proofread to be sure that you've divided it into two words. Remember that *lot* is a noun, a separate word, and *a* is simply the article modifying it. Look at these two sentences: "My church owns a good deal of property. My church owns a lot of property." You don't run together the spelling of "a good deal"; neither do you run together "a lot."

Disinterested/uninterested: Many people use these words interchangeably, but in fact they have distinct meanings. To be *uninterested* in something is to be bored by it; to be *disinterested* is to have nothing at stake, to be impartial. Thus, we would expect judges to be *disinterested* in cases before them, but we would certainly not expect them to be *uninterested.*

Escape: Some people pronounce this as though it begins with *ex* instead of *es.* It doesn't, so don't.

Et cetera: This is a Latin term meaning "and so on." It's two separate words, abbreviated "etc." Occasionally people misspell it, reversing the "t" and "c." (You'll avoid that problem if you remember the Latin.) People more often make mistakes in pronouncing this term than in writing it. A well-educated man of my acquaintance always says "eck-cetera." Don't be like him. Another common error with this abbreviation is prefacing it with *and.* Since the term itself includes *and,* it is a mistake to say "and et cetera."

Flaunt/flout: These words sound somewhat alike but have different meanings. To *flaunt* something is to display it ostentatiously: "He flaunted his good fortune by buying a Porsche." To *flout,* on the other hand, is to disregard something scornfully: "He flouted convention by coming to the formal reception in a sweatsuit."

Imply/infer: To *imply* is to suggest indirectly or hint; to *infer* is to take the hint.

Irregardless: This is a common misconstruing of *regardless,* which means "without regard to," so adding a prefixing negative to the word is not necessary.

Lie/lay/laid: Probably ninety-nine percent of the population makes errors with these verb forms. But someone in your congregation undoubtedly knows the correct forms and will regard you more highly if you do too. So here we go. The problem with the *lie/lay* distinction is that there are actually two different verbs, *to lie* and *to lay,* and they each have different principal parts. "Principal parts" should echo in your minds from grade-school years, but let me remind you that a verb has three principal parts: the form that goes with the infinitive, the simple past tense, and the past participle (the form that goes with a "helping verb"). Thus, principal parts of *to write* are *write, wrote, written*. Now, back to *lie* and *lay*. *To lie* is an intransitive verb; it does not have an object. We use it to refer to animate things, like ourselves: "I was just about to lie down for a nap when the phone rang." The past tense of the verb is *lay:* "I lay tossing in bed for three hours, unable to sleep," and the past participle is *lain:* "My dog has lain in that same spot for hours." The other verb, *to lay*, is transitive; it takes an object. The principal parts of the verb are *lay, laid,* and *laid:* "Just lay the book on my desk." "I laid the book on the coffee table." "I've laid down all my burdens." *Hint: Notice that the spelling is "laid," not "layed."*

Literally: This word means that something is truly the case, that not just an image is meant. If I say that I was so happy that I literally walked ten feet off the ground, I'm misusing the word, unless of course I am a saint who can levitate! Many people use *literally* as a word of emphasis, which is a misuse. We have many words of emphasis; to misuse *literally* as one of them is to denigrate its real meaning.

Than/then: Than is used for comparisons: "Matthew's gospel is longer than Mark's." *Then* is an adverb having to do with time or consequence: "Then he said to them all, 'If any want to become my followers, let them deny themselves and take up their cross daily and follow me'" (Lk. 9:23). In this context, you probably know the difference between *then* and *than.* In writing, however, it is easy to mistake one for the other. Proofreading is the key.

Their/there/they're: Most English teachers could retire if they had a dollar for every time they've marked mistakes in the use of these words. *Their* is a plural possessive pronoun: "Their disciples believed they had lost their master." *There* is occasionally an adverb ("Put your books over there") but is more often a placeholder at the beginning of a sentence: "There are two main reasons for my belief." *They're* is a contraction for *they are.* Again, proofreading is the key. Because the most common problem is the substitution of *there* for the other two words, do a search for that word in your papers and check to see that each use is correct.

Your/you're: The first is the possessive pronoun: "You left your book in my car." The second is a contraction for "you are": "You're going to be late for church if you don't hurry." Because we pronounce both the same, it's very easy to make errors in their written use.

A Glossary of Commonly Misspelled Words

Spell-check functions on computers are a real gift from God for those of us whose are orthographically challenged! In spite of that device, however, spelling errors do still crop up. This section will list some of the most common and suggest some ways to help you improve. But if you are a congenitally weak speller, you may take some comfort from two thoughts: First, researchers have found that the ability to spell is unrelated to other forms of intelligence; second, as someone once said, it's a mighty poor mind that can think of only one way to spell a word!

Accommodations: In ads for hotels and such, you'll often see this one misspelled, with the second *m* omitted. Remember that your *accommodations* will have a *commode*, and maybe you'll recall the second *m*.

Attendance: There seems little logic behind *ence* and *ance* endings: You just have to learn which is which. However, my third-grade teacher, Mrs. Ward, told our class that you *attend* a *dance*, and that little aid always helps me recall the correct spelling of the word.

Beginning: We commonly double the consonant before adding *ing* if the vowel is soft. Note the difference between the soft *o* in *hop* and the hard *o* in *hope;* doubling the consonant gives us *hopping*, while dropping the *e* and adding *ing* produces *hoping.*

Business: For some reason, this word just about tops the charts for misspelling. Think of it as *busyness* with the *y* changed to an *i*, and you'll get it right.

Definite: This word has as its root *finite.* You wouldn't misspell that one, so remember the root and you'll get *definite* right also.

Incidentally: This is one of many words ending with the adverbial *ly.* Be aware that if the root word ends with an *l*, we still add the *ly.*

It's/its: We've considered this confusion in the section on apostrophes, but it's worth reviewing: Remember that *it's* is a contraction for *it is* or *it has,* while *its* is a possessive pronoun; this sentence gives an example of its use.

Less/fewer and *amount/number:* In formal speech and writing, we use *less* and *amount* to refer to items that are not delineated by numbers; therefore, we would say "less money" but "fewer dollars"and "amount of cash" but "number of contributions."

Loose/lose: Frequently, people write *loose,* an adjective, when they intend *lose,* a verb: "The little girl is about to *lose* her *loose* tooth."

Occasion: Writers often double the wrong letter here. I don't know any mnemonic aids for this one, but if you look at it and write or type it out correctly several times, you can effectively retrain your brain to get it right.

Occurred: Get this one right by thinking about the pronunciation. If you omit the second *r,* as many do, then it would be pronounced like *cured.* And it isn't, so don't!

Separate: For some reason, this word leads the pack when it comes to misspelling. Most writers seem to want to make the first *a* into an *e.* I've always found mnemonic aids to be helpful, so let me share with you what an elementary-school teacher, Mrs. Ward, once told me: "There is *a rat* in *separate.*" Silly as it sounds, it may help you remember the correct spelling.

Stationery/stationary: One of these words is a noun meaning the materials you use in letter writing, and the other is an adjective meaning "stable." How to tell which is which? I can't imagine that we used these words a lot in third grade, but I do recall it was once again Mrs. Ward who offered the device to solve this one: Station*ery,* she said, is mostly pap*er.*

Weather/whether: Weather has to do with rain and snow; *whether* is a conjunction that introduces choices: "I don't know whether to go or stay." If you confuse the spelling of these, remember that you *wear* a coat in bad *weather.*

Were/where: Depending on *where* you come from, you may pronounce these words the same way and therefore confuse their spellings. If you can recall the *wh* sound, you won't make the mistake. Again, proofreading is your key.

Who's/whose: The first is a contraction for *who is* or *who has,* while the second is the possessive form of *who* or *which.* Compare "I don't know who's teaching that class" with "I don't know whose backpack it is."

Writing: Some people misspell this by doubling the *t.* Be aware that we have a hard *i* and therefore need the single *t* to keep it that way. Of course, *written* has the double *t* and the soft *i* sound.

Further Resources

Hult, Christine A., and Thomas N. Huckin. *The New Century Handbook.* Boston: Allyn & Bacon, 1999.

_____. *The New Century Handbook.* CD-ROM. Boston: Allyn & Bacon, 2000.

Sbaratta, Philip. *GrammarCoach.* Diskette. Vers. 1.0. Boston: Allyn & Bacon, 1998.

Scharton, Maurice, and Janice Neulieb. *Things Your Grammar Never Told You.* Boston: Allyn & Bacon, 1999.

APPENDIX 1

Using Inclusive Language

Inclusive language can be a hot-button issue in religious and secular settings today, and it is not my purpose to enter the fray concerning the arguments for and against. Instead, I want to share some thoughts about how you can create inclusive language if you want or need to work at that. Inclusive language is not at all hard to achieve. Many of you probably already use such language appropriately and steadily. If you are still struggling with this issue, let's take a little time to think about how we can make these changes in our speech and writing.

Such changes can be done gracefully, leaving us with a style equal to or even superior to our earlier tone. For one thing, when we revise for inclusiveness, we are, after all, revising—and revising, as you know by now, is at the very heart of effective writing (see chapter 2). Let's look at a few examples of inclusive language issues. Using noninclusive language, we might write this: "If a student wishes to register for my class, he should see me immediately." To make such a sentence inclusive, we have several options. One that we often unconsciously choose is to use *they* instead of *he*. Of course, such a substitution creates what most people regard as a grammatical error: *they* is plural, not singular, so using *they* creates an error of agreement between the noun (*student*) and the pronoun (*they*).

One correct option is substituting *he or she*. Our sentence now reads, "If a student wishes to register for my class, he or she should see me immediately." That's not bad; however, many folks will find the *he or she* structure to be cumbersome. Some people write *he/she* or *s/he*. Such "slash words" have the advantage of being shorter than *he or she*, but some find them awkward or odd. Two better options are these: "Any student wishing to register for my class should see me immediately" and "Students wishing to register for my class should see me immediately." Both of these have the advantage of being tighter, simpler sentences than the original one, and therefore are not only inclusive but stylistically better. The second one would probably be my choice because it suggests that more than one student will be seeing me, and if I'm expecting more than one, it seems more accurate to say so.

A second (and thornier) issue is inclusive language as it relates to God. This issue is complicated and divisive, but we cannot and should not avoid it. For some people, God as Father says it all; biblical and traditional witness to such language is adequate and persuasive. Others, however, need alternative language. Perhaps they have had such negative experiences of a father that "God the Father" is not a comforting or loving image. Also, many have found that traditional "God language" such as King, Master, or Lord suggests a magisterial God more interested in ruling than in loving and sustaining, a God whose names implicitly support our unfortunate human impulse to rule others and exploit the environment. If we think of ourselves as created in the image of God, the language with which we describe God will reflect our own aspirations. Bringing some of those unconscious assumptions to our consciousness for a thoughtful critiquing is certainly a good effect of any meditation upon our language choices.

In such a complex and even emotion-fraught area, it is certainly not my purpose to advocate one point of view over another, but rather to offer the writer/speaker some choices. So let's look at the language available. A friend of mine, a priest, has told me that in his own spiritual life, God is always Father: This terminology results from his training but also from his own experiences of deep prayer. However, he recognizes that in his public prayer, he is heard by many for whom that language cannot lead to deeper spirituality. So when he is praying publicly, speaking the community's prayers as it were, he chooses to address God as "Creator God" or "Loving Savior." A woman I know, a Protestant lay pastor, prays both publicly and privately to the "Holy One." When I asked her about her choice of title for God, she told me that "Holy One" was the least idolatrous term she could find; she said that labeling God is always a bit dangerous because in doing so, we hem God in, not with the narrowness of language, which is, after all, God's gift, but with our sometimes ideological and narrow construction of meaning.

The great Anglican thinker and writer Charles Williams constantly found new ways of understanding God through language.[1] For example, he thought and wrote of Christ as *Messias*, the Greek spelling serving as a fresh image for him. God was "the Protection" or "the Mercy." Using these traditional yet somewhat different terms was what he needed to do to appropriate the Christian tradition for himself. If you read about Williams' impact on many of his readers, you'll learn that he (along with C. S. Lewis) was responsible for many skeptics' and seekers' finding their way to Christianity. I suspect that Williams' fresh approach to language played no small role in that pathway to conversion. He and the great poets like Donne, Herbert, and Hopkins, who have struggled with the inadequacy of words to tell of God, remind me to be humble in what language I use or recommend for speaking and writing about God. When we write about God, we are privileged to be articulating wonder. We should always be aware of the holy ground and never be too confident that ours is the only way or only right way.

When we talk about inclusive language, gender inclusivity is usually what we have in mind. However, traditional language choices have often excluded in ways other than gender. For example, when we refer to someone who can't or won't

---

[1]Williams (1886–1945) develops his religious ideas in a number of fascinating novels, including *Many Dimensions, Shadows of Ecstasy*, and *The Place of the Lion*. He was a member of a literary circle, called the Inklings, which included C. S. Lewis, Dorothy Sayers, and J. R. R. Tolkien. For more information, see Humphrey Carpenter's study, *The Inklings* (Boston: Houghton Mifflin, 1978) or visit an Inklings Web site, www.geocities.com/Athens/7734/inklings.htm.

understand the truth of a given situation, how do we describe the person? Often, we say that the person is *blind.* Such word choice may seem unexceptional to those of us who currently enjoy the sense of sight, but to those who do not have that gift, the use of *blind* as a metaphor is not so harmless. One of our most popular Christian hymns, "Amazing Grace," may be heard as perpetuating the suggestion of "blind" as evil, or at least as a condition of one's life before accepting Christ: "Was blind but now I see." What are we to do with such images, especially considering that they do seem to be scriptural in their bases?

I can't claim a comprehensive answer to these questions, and I think that our being bothered by them is the appropriate cost of being people of conscience and people of prayer. If we ask ourselves the important questions, "What is the compassionate and Christian choice?" and "What words will lead my hearers or readers to a deeper spirituality?" the answer may well become clearer, if only case by case. A contemporary gospel singer, Marsha Stevens, has recorded a collection of traditional hymns offered in inclusive language: She revises the troubling line in "Amazing Grace" as "Was bound but now am free."[2] This particular solution seems theologically and pastorally sound to me; the language of unbinding and freeing surely has profound scriptural resonance.

We also need to be aware of the impact of word choices regarding images of light and dark. How often do we hear or say things like "It was a dark day," "He committed a black deed," or "She tried to blacken my name"? Such oppositional language, we all know by now, is rightly offensive to people of color. Nonetheless, we often just slide into it by default. With a heightened awareness, however, we can catch and revise such negative language and say what we mean. If it was an "evil day" or if someone tries to "ruin our name," we can simply say so.

But these are just a few answers to a few questions of language use. Inevitably, more will arise, and answers won't always come easily. Language is a gift that may divide as well as

---

[2]Marsha Stevens, "For Those Who Know It Best: Inclusive Hymns for the Church" (Costa Mesa: Balm Publishing, 1995), compact disc.

unite us. It can emphasize our differences instead of bridging them. The only real answer will be in our ongoing desire to speak and write with humility and God-centeredness, and to do so even when it takes extra effort. The essayist George Orwell once wrote, "Let the meaning choose the word, and not the other way about."[3]

Sometimes, though, it *is* our meaning that presents a problem, and our language is simply following along. However, language does serve to reinforce meaning, and we need to consider the consequences of our speech and writing. An example of this sort of situation is what I call the "man who" sentence. I once served on a search committee with an individual who shared his ideas about the kind of departmental chair we were seeking: "We want a man who can do...a man who thinks...a man who will lead..." You get the picture. This person was indeed letting his meaning choose his words. The problem was that he had not really examined what he meant. He did not consciously intend to exclude women, but the idea of a male departmental chair was comfortable for him, and therefore his language revealed what he thought and felt. When his language was challenged and altered, so were his assumptions. In such situations, hard though it may be, a group or committee may need to make ground rules about language use. And beginning with *chair* instead of *chairman* (or the awkward *chairperson*) is always a good idea.

Once we start to think about how our language choices include or exclude, more and more issues and examples will come to mind. A friend of mine, a laywoman very active in her church, recently went to a spiritual growth committee meeting at which the committee chair suggested that the committee might sponsor several programs, each one to be organized by "a couple." My friend is single, and she felt immediately excluded from the plans. When she told the group how she felt, the chair responded that she had not really meant "a couple"–any two people could team up and work together–but my friend still felt somewhat disenfranchised, and understandably so.

---

[3]George Orwell, "Politics and the English Language," in *Shooting an Elephant and Other Essays* (New York: Harcourt, 1945), 91.

Our churches often use "family" language, which has the effect of excluding singles. While families certainly need to be recognized and supported in every way, singles also are a viable part of the church community, and they need to be treated as such.

When we speak as though everyone were white, or physically able, or part of a traditional family, or male, we need to listen to ourselves and ask how we can do better at proclaiming the real, inclusive gospel of Jesus. If our *meaning* is love and inclusivity, our words *should and must* follow. In doing the hard work of caring for our language as part of how we share the good news, we will deal more respectfully with all our brothers and sisters, and we will live lives more deeply faithful to the gospel.

APPENDIX 2

Writing Essay Exams

Many capable students struggle with essay exams, and many faculty struggle with reading the outcome of their students' labors. Is this because the students aren't capable or haven't studied? No. There is skill involved in taking essay exams, and a lot of students do themselves a disservice by failing to acquire or use this skill. Also, sometimes the essay exam creates a certain level of anxiety among those not confident of their writing skills. Regardless of how you respond to the exam situation, it's always good to approach it (as all else) with prayer. *Holy God, keep us in your care as we take this test. Please let those who are anxious feel your reassuring touch. Let us remember that you are why we do this and all else.*

With that foundation, let's take a look at the special writing circumstances posed by the essay exam.

We spent a good deal of time in chapter 2 looking at how we can create central ideas in writing. Well, the good news is that essay exams essentially hand us our central ideas. We don't have to meander about in our minds, wondering what in the world to write about or how best to show our knowledge. All we have to do is use our knowledge to develop those ideas. In writing essay exams, we identify key words and phrases that tell us what to do. It's important that we take what we are given, read carefully, and respond appropriately to the question as asked.

Here's a typical essay question from a church history class: "Discuss the effects of Constantine's conversion on the church of the fourth and fifth centuries. Point out both positive and negative effects." After reading this question, what's the first thing you do? Start writing? You only have a certain amount of time, so you think fast, *Um, let's see—well, the end of the persecutions—yes, very big effect of Constantine's conversion. Right.* And so you start writing about the end of persecutions, and that leads you to writing about how the desert fathers got started, and you write and write, and it all is true and good, and you really know a lot about this stuff! Whew! Great! But then you get the test back and find out you did poorly because you didn't address the question. But you *knew* that stuff! What went wrong? Well, one thing that went wrong was that you wrote a discourse on the rise of the desert fathers, with only a passing initial reference to Constantine. Off-center responses can account for many low grades.

When we look at an essay question, we are often tempted to answer with the first idea that comes to mind. We feel under the pressure of time, and we want to get going. So as soon as we think of something—anything—to say in response, we're off to the races. Bad idea! Perhaps the most important time you spend on an essay exam is the time *before* actually writing the essay. Here's how it should go:

First, you need to *check out the whole test.* Notice if you are offered choices, such as "Answer no. 1, and then answer either no. 2 or no. 3." Notice the distribution of points, if any. Sometimes a test will ask you to answer all questions, but the first two are worth 25 points each, and the third, 50. Common sense dictates that your response to the last question should be about the length of the first two combined, but if you start with the first and ignore time constraints, you may end up with only a short time left to deal with the third, most important question. So scope out the whole test and *plan how to use your time most effectively.* Then go to the first question.

Begin by *reading the question with care,* paying attention to what it does and does not ask. *Look carefully at the verbs.* Verbs tell you what to do in the essay. Common verbs in essay questions are *discuss, defend, explain, trace, analyze,* and *define.* Do what the verb tells you to do. Don't just "trace" if you are asked to "defend." Most teachers spend a good deal of time wording the sentences to encourage the best responses. Don't let their work go to waste.

Next, *look for the scope of the question, including key words.* Notice that in the example above, you're asked to look at fourth- and fifth-century effects on the church, so you don't need to think about Constantine's lingering effect in the sixth or sixteenth centuries. Also, the question asks you to cite positive and negative effects. Don't get so involved in discussing one that you forget the other. Now that you've examined the question, you need to *jot down key ideas to develop.* For this question, you need to be sure to address positive and negative effects, so start by jotting down one of each. Just a key word or two will do. Spend a couple of minutes on this process. Then—don't start writing quite yet! There's just another minute's worth of work to do before you write, and that minute will make your essay a whole lot better.

Look at the little list you've just created and think about how to present it. You are writing an essay exam, and you should do your best to *make it a real, organized essay,* with a beginning, middle, and end. In chapter 2, we discussed order of emphasis. You can use this method to good effect as a simple organizing device for your essay exam. Let's say that you glance at what you've noted and are impressed with the positives about Constantine's conversion. You'll want to begin, then, with the negatives, because it's best to lead to the stronger points. Make a note of that on your list. Then choose the strongest positive you've noted, and circle that as your ending. You've now created a rough but workable outline. Now you can start writing.

You decide to begin with a very short funnel paragraph (see chapter 2) and follow it with the negatives you've listed, *using appropriate, key, supportive details.* Then you create a transitional sentence, something like "But in spite of these negative aspects of Constantine's conversion, the positive aspects are more outstanding." Then you go through those, saving the most important one for last. You begin that final example with another quick transition, "However, the most positive outcome was…" Then explain it and finally *offer some sense of an ending;* here, you might conclude by reiterating, "In this way, Constantine's impact most strongly shaped the age."

Let's try another one. Again, the question is from a church history class: "Those who came to America to escape persecution or to seek a new life of freedom brought with them the old problems from Europe. What were some of these problems? Explain how they were or were not handled any better in the 'New World.'"

Examining this question, we should notice that it has three distinct sentences, and each calls for attention. And we need to remember that our goal is to show through our answer that we do indeed know something about church history. This question allows us to show some of our knowledge about "the old problems" of Europe as well as church history in America. But it is a big question, and if we don't focus well, we can either be overwhelmed by its scope, or we can ramble around the question to no good effect. So we reread the question and decide what our reading and thinking leads us to want to argue. "What were the old problems?" is obviously the first question to approach. We decide to focus on ethnocentrism and denominationalism, which certainly led to big problems in the New World. And because both of these grow out of human pride, we think we will begin with that point. But then there is the final question, "Were these problems handled better in the so-called New World?" Well, yes. "Explain how" is next. What we've read and learned makes it clear that the simple fact of space in America was key: We could always get away from one another and found independent communities of like-minded folk. Many examples come to mind, and we jot several down. At this point, it's good to check back and be sure we're on target in answering the question as asked, so we check out our details. All of them give evidence of the "Old World" problems appearing in the "New World" and being handled better here; everything that we're planning to say, therefore, will be answering the exam question appropriately. But is this all we need to say? We don't want to get bogged down so much in one aspect of the answer that we miss something big. As we review the question, it occurs to us that we must say something about the concept of freedom of religion in America and how it helped us avoid some of those problems. Reviewing again, we notice that we have written only about America, as though it were all of the

"New World." We need to rethink the response and add some thoughts about the rest of the hemisphere! Having thought, planned, and checked, we write the response. And we're done.

Well, almost done. On essay exams, it is important to watch the time carefully, *always saving time at the end—the more, the better—for some revising and proofreading.* In a writing such as this, you and I don't have time for a lot of rethinking or the activities we associate with global revision. But we can do something, and in revising, something is always better than nothing. Taking the final moments to reread the essay, we may have time to add substantive comments, even stick a sentence between the lines, adding an important detail that escaped us as we wrote. We may decide to cross out an irrelevant detail or stick in a transitional word that gives improved flow to the essay. At the very least, we can check for omitted words, obvious misspellings, or punctuation and grammar errors.

Time's up, and NOW you're done! And I'll bet you did fine.